30
YEARS
OF TRAINSPOTTING

(*Frontispiece*) What it was all about. Derby Open Day 30 August 1958 and I stand (aged 15), with cousin David and Uncle George, alongside 'Britannia' 70017 *Arrow*. The size and majesty of the engines, plus being able to get so close to them, was part of the magic of the day, as well as being able to record so many numbers on shed and Works. 92166 stands behind, host to small boys. HORACE STRETTON

30
YEARS
OF TRAINSPOTTING

(DON'T FORGET YOUR ANARAK)

JOHN STRETTON

Unicorn Books

With thanks to the rest of the Gang of Four

Front cover Taken twenty years apart, these two views evidence the enduring lure of railways. (*Top*) In the happy days when steam still ran on the Isle of Wight, a young spotter seems oblivious to the summer rain, as he studies the front-end of SR 02 0-4-4T No 21 *Sandown* at Ventnor, on 24 August 1965.

In contrast, (*Bottom*) the sun shines brilliantly on the author's family, as they admire 50007 *Sir Edward Elgar* at Reading Open Day, 1 June 1985.

Back cover A photograph that tells some of the story. Despite the rain, the crowd on the platform waits in eager anticipation, as ER A1 No 60114 *W. P. Allen* draws into Derby Midland station to make a once-only trip to Worcester, with the Derbyshire Railway Society. The 'unlucky' ones can only watch from the adjacent platforms, 12 July 1964.

Other titles by the same author
Steam on Shed, Blandford Press
Leicestershire Railway memories, Unicorn Books

Other titles in the Unicorn Railway series
Midland through the Peak by Brian Radford
Great Central Rail Tour by John M. C. Healy
Cotswold Memories by Dennis Edwards and Ron Pigram

First published in 1990 by
UNICORN BOOKS,
16 Laxton Gardens,
Paddock Wood,
Kent TN12 6BB

© M. John Stretton 1990

British Library Cataloguing in Publication Data
Stretton, John
    30 years of trainspotting
    1. Great Britain. Railway services, history –
    I. Title
    385′.092′4

    ISBN 1-85241-006-X

Typeset by Vitaset, Paddock Wood.
Printed by Netherwood Dalton & Co Ltd Huddersfield.

CONTENTS

The Gang of Four! Clockwise from top left, Les, David, Pete
and myself stand proudly with Standard Class 4 2-6-4T
No 80008, on Corkerhill shed, in the late evening light of
24th August, 1964.

FOREWORD

If you were to ask me – and many friends have over the years – what it is about railways that fascinates and hooks me, I could not give a rational answer. The same would apply to my other long-standing passion, the music of Duane Eddy. But perhaps it is as well that a clinical explanation cannot be given; surely, it is better to feel the thing deeply and sincerely and accept it, rather than explain it away. Certainly, the love of both trains and twang is deep-seated and enduring, much to the occasional annoyance and bewilderment of those close to me. The two subjects actually came together on a number of occasions – but more of that later!

One of the attractions of collecting anything is the hope and the chance of coming across something unusual, rare, or exciting. With railways, possibly due to the sheer size, complexity and uncertainty of the operation, the possibilities are ever-present and it is not uncommon to chance on some rare working or brand new development, or the like. Indeed, the unexpected in railway operation is constantly there for the seasoned eye, although the very rare event – the 'mint coin' – is given only to a few.

For me, one of the overriding joys of trainspotting – for I do still collect those numbers although the photographs are now *the* important thing – is the peace I experience at the lineside. For some, it is fishing, reading or even a Hamlet cigar! But put me at the side of a railway line and I am happy. Almost, there is no need for an actual train, the place is therapeutic enough; lineside beats librium any day!

At the close of 1986, I had completed thirty years of this love affair, with my passion still as ardent as ever. Over the years, I have seen many and varied sights and events, with not a few being rare, strange, humorous or merely interesting; in this volume, I have tried to pass on some of the enjoyment and recreation – and scrapes – that I have experienced. Set out in chronological form, each chapter tells the story first, then shows what is talked about in accompanying illustrations. These have come from a number of sources and I must take this opportunity to thank all those who so readily put their work at my disposal and gave so freely of their time, help and advice; in particular, Horace Gamble and Geoff King, whose photos I am proud to include. Also, a great vote of thanks must go to Messrs. Elliff & Co, in Doncaster, and Paul at Freezeframe in Gloucester, for their not inconsiderable help in resurrecting something printable from some distinctly dodgy negatives; to the Publishers, for having the foresight to have faith in the project; Hugh Ramsey for his ready and cheerful help and inspiration; David Richards, for putting up with the occasional diesel sorties and for pulling a few strings; to my parents, for enduring and aiding my obsession, often to their own discomfort; but above all to my wife and family for their patience. As with any passion, there are victims on the sidelines; those who get crushed in the single-minded pursuit. They have borne with it, with usually little more than grumbles, and I have been able to indulge myself. To Judith, Adam and Tammy – a big, big 'Thank you'! You'll never know how much it's meant!

Finally, all photos are taken by me, unless otherwise stated.

John Stretton
January 1989

CHAPTER ONE

'No, you cannot have an Ian Allan spotter's book!'

This was Dad's reaction, at the beginning of 1956, when I asked him for such a book. Not that he was against trains, it was just that I picked up a new hobby every three weeks – or so it seemed to him! – and then dropped it just as quickly, but first having bought all the gear for it, and he thought that this trainspotting lark was as transitory as the rest. Thirty years on, I think I have proved him wrong!

The bug actually bit midway through 1955, deceptively quietly, when 'Jubilee' 45636 *Uganda* rolled gently to a stop, one afternoon, in Loughborough station, sixteen miles to the north of Leicester, on a Manchester-bound express. In those days, I travelled to school by train, from Syston to Loughborough and, this day, on my way home, waiting for our local service, some of my colleagues already had the spotting habit and I thought, 'Why not join them?' I took that number and all the others from then on and began writing them down in an exercise book. Very soon, however, the columns were overrunning each other and the pages were looking messy and getting out of hand. What I really needed was an Ian Allan spotter's book, so that I could see just what I was after. 'It really is essential, Dad, Honest!' Eventually, seeing that this hobby was lasting longer than the others, he relented and I got my book – and I have never looked back.

Closely following *Uganda* was 'Stanier' 2-6-2T 40182, at the head of our local service; and then, on the way home, there was a succession of freights, hauled by either 'Garratts' or 'Stanier' 8F 2-8-0s, known to us as 'Consols'. From these, it became clear that all the numbers started with a 4 and, thus, guided by my contemporaries, I needed an Ian Allan's *Midland ABC*. Having eventually bought this, I was somewhat bemused when I saw that the engines on the Great Central line which crossed Loughborough station at the southern platform end began with a 6! Having then graduated to an *Eastern ABC*, the next step was a Combined volume, covering all regions and including the few diesels then around, from which, to my horror, I saw that there were literally thousands of engines. My natural instinct was to want to see them all; but with well over 20,000 in the book, just what had I started?

In retrospect, Loughborough was an excellent place to start, in the middle of England, where a wide variety of engines might be seen. There were those literal strings of freights, as I travelled between Syston and school, but more especially, as well as the Midland main line with its own excitement, there was the Great Central crossing that main line as already mentioned. And next to the Midland station, the Brush Engineering Works, where new British Railways diesels – later to become Class 31 and 47, as well as the odd prototype and foreign builds – were being constructed and often could be seen, ready to leave the Works' complex. I didn't know it then, but I was being given a dream start to my hobby.

Fairly soon, I was spending all my spare time a quarter-of-a-mile from home, at Thurmaston, at one of two bridges, watching the trains go by – and consequently being late home for meals, bed, etc. There always seemed to be a train in the distance when I should be making tracks for home and I just had to wait for it to come! This activity was interspersed by one or two trips to Leicester Midland sheds (code 15C) where, in company with a lot of other like-minded kids, I tried to see the engines in the shed yard, from the 'Birdcage' – the footpath area between the Mental Hospital, the terraced houses in Hutchinson Street and the railway. On my first visits, it was necessary to somehow clamber up the fence, constructed from old sleepers but, by 1958, this had been replaced by iron railings – which are still there to this day. Rumour was that a child had fallen off the sleepers and had been badly injured, hence the change; but whether this was true I know not.

Not long after this, I and cousin David – who by this time had also been bitten by the bug – together with one or two other friends, started hankering after pastures new; and one of our very first trips was to Rugby, by train, over the Midland line from Leicester, now, sadly, long since gone. My records for this first trip are sketchy, but I recall that immediately we arrived at Rugby station a 'Semi' ('Coronation' Class) with a sloping front end (legacy of the streamlining) went roaring through the station, northbound on the fast avoiding line, but behind some coaches that were in the platform. I know not to this day which engine this was, but it was certainly the only one I saw in this state! The delights were many and varied that day and I could hardly contain my excitement, as we rushed about the platform scribbling furiously the numbers of the trains that seemed almost continuous. But some highlights do stand out: such as a brief cab-ride along a bay platform, on B1 61282; the juxtaposition of modern SR diesel 10203 and aged steam 58293; the sight and sound of the 'Semis'; and my first unrebuilt 'Patriot', 45505 *The Royal Army Ordnance Corps*. We all went home exhausted but happy!

As we did on trips to Nuneaton and Grantham, the latter reached by bus. The first trip here, on 26 July 1956, was just as much an eye-opener as Rugby, with the delights this time being the 'Gresley Pacifics' and the fascination of watching engines turn on a triangle at the rear of the shed, rather than on a turntable. By now, wherever I went, even family trips to, say, Nottingham, or the school trip to London, I was hanging out of carriage windows, collecting numbers – much to the irritation of parents and teachers! And as often as possible, during school lunch-break, a few of us would practise our 4min miling, to reach the Central station in Loughborough to see the southbound *South Yorkshireman*. Always, in my experience, an A3, there were regulars and 60102 *Sir Frederick Banbury*, 60104 *Solario*, and 60111 *Enterprise* became 'old friends'. Having seen the train, we would then sprint back to school, to slump in an exhausted, sweaty heap for the rest of the afternoon!

By the end of 1957, the school had moved to the outskirts of Loughborough and we now went by bus; and I only saw the very occasional trip freight here, on the ex-LNW line that ran alongside the school field, not long before the line closed. To keep my hand in, I joined a trainspotting club – the Attenborough Model Railway Club, based in Nottingham. Not, on the face of it a logical choice, but it came highly recommended and I was not disappointed. My first trip with them was to the sheds of the Nottingham area, on 10 March 1957. I was so looking forward to it, but the heavens opened and treated us to weather so common to trainspotting – it rained constantly all day! Even inside some of the sheds we were barely sheltered. Mansfield, especially, seemed to have as much sky as roof, with my notebook becoming very bedraggled from sooty drips as we walked round! Colwick (then 38A), was the undoubted highlight, with what seemed a bewildering array of engines, 109 of which (of 110 on shed) were new to me:

90303	64739	63699	63754	90136	90064	68601
64257	63675	90118	61896	64832	68629	90166
64199	64267	61056	64248	64980	64762	63674
68887	90161	63657	63729	90189	63694	63614
64221	61833	61915	64747	64345	90036	64388
90146	90618	61814	63688	67788	61726	90476
90473	90432	64438	63839	67799	61768	90634
90115	64195	63829	90460	64178	69810	68851
68927	61888	61870	64988	67760	61821	90002
90073	61763	90263	61804	90130	90103	90037
61768	90015	68785	61824	61974	63873	68863
68550	61873	90629	64798	90218	61738	61732
61947	90083	68871	64813	90139	90185	64183
63816	68829	64763	64420	64238	69804	68950
61160	61777	63587	90084	61771	69812	90394
67751	61982	64269	90215	68768		

But if I thought that was a lot, I was literally speechless at the number we saw at Stratford (30A), not long afterwards. On an AMR train trip, by way of Leicester (Midland) and Kentish Town, to reach Stratford, I had heard that the shed had the largest allocation in the country, but I never expected to see 251 on one shed! There was everything, from 'Britannias' to old ER faithfuls awaiting scrap, to Departmentals, to diesels – and even GWR 9401! After this trip was logged in my ABC, I had seen 2,718 different engines in less than two years, with 1,742 of them being Midland engines – and only 17 Western, mostly seen at Leicester (Central) on the York-Bournemouth services. The latter though was very soon to change!

In August 1957 the family went on holiday to Dawlish Warren. We couldn't walk down to the beach without seeing, it seemed, at least half-a-dozen expresses as well as locals and freights! My insatiable appetite was both partly satisfied, but also whetted in equal measure – due largely to parental rationing of trainspotting time. Nevertheless, with only limited access, my cops tally rose by 255 – 245 of them Western.

After this, trips came thick and fast, with another memorable one being the AMR trip to London sheds on 20 April 1958. David, especially, was excited at seeing 70004 *William Shakespeare* on Stewart's Lane shed; so much so, that he chased after it as it prepared to leave the shed yard. The tour leader, affectionately known as 'Gumboot'(!), was decidedly concerned, but with a limp and being mute he was no match for an athletic youngster! And then came Derby Open Day on 30 August.

For those of us living in the East Midlands this was one of the highlights of the year. It had the perfect combination of displaying specially gathered engines which were on show for the enthusiasts to view and 'climb on', an entry to the Works without previously arranged permits and a chance to see all manner of engines within the Works' confines – engines from other parts of the country, those in for attention, older ones awaiting scrapping and even bits of those already having received the attentions of the cutter's torch – and to be able to wander around looking at all this, totally at your own leisure. Needless to say, the event was packed every year. This was the first major event at which I used my camera – a Kodak Brownie 127, that had been given to me not long beforehand. Until then, any photos I had taken had been with Dad's camera and only with his express permission and supervision. Unfortunately, his camera was superior to mine, but I snapped away without thinking about this, or realising the inbuilt deficiencies of the lens and set focal and shutter speed. Looking back at those shots now, I am gravely disappointed at the lack of focal length, but I knew no better in those days, nor could I afford anything of higher quality, had I been more knowledgeable. Some of the problems can be seen in Plates 7 & 8; my attempts at shooting the *Thames-Clyde Express* at speed, with a double-headed 'Jubilee', will ever remain in my own files!

1959 continued much as before, with trips far and

wide, but also highlights 'at home', one of the latter being the sight of double-headed Metrovick diesels on the 'Condor' express freight, British Railways' new Anglo-Scottish container freight, from Hendon to Gushetfaulds (Glasgow) – and return. It was the fastest freight train in the country, making the longest non-stop freight run and with the locos making the longest through run in BR rosters, and it was a daily excitement. Another was a non-railway excitement. Having arrived back at Leicester (London Road) station, after a day trip to London, world class boxer Willie Pastrano was on the same train. A starry-eyed kid, I pushed my way through to him (with some help from Dad) and thrust my trainspotting book at him, for his autograph – that signature still resides on a clear page of its own, amidst hundreds of engine numbers on the surrounding pages!

Holidays that year were at Caister, near Yarmouth. The M&GN Joint line north from Yarmouth Beach, through Caister, was in its death throes – having been closed as a line on 28 February – and I count myself lucky that I saw it that summer, albeit briefly, with a small number of engineers' trains. Sadly, my photos leave something to be desired, as do those taken at Yarmouth (South Town) on my sorties to 'bunk' the shed. But, undoubtedly, *the* highlight of the year was the AMR train trip to Swindon and Eastleigh – *The Eastlindon Flyer* of 20 September.

Swindon was an oft-read-about dream and the sense of anticipation was almost painful, it was so intense. Fortunately, I was not to be disappointed; and even Eastleigh was a magic place, almost matching Swindon for pleasure and excitement that day. The whole spectrum was seen, from lines of engines awaiting scrap, to brand new engines, both diesel and steam and I am forever glad that I took a shot of 92212, brand new, not yet delivered to its depot, standing in the sunshine, in Swindon Works' yard. Sadly, my attempt at snapping *Boxhill* in Eastleigh Works' yard was not successful; I needed a new camera – and that was forthcoming at Christmas 1959.

I became the proud owner of a Halina A1; still fixed shutter speed, but bigger sized negatives and much, much improved focal length. The results were much more to my liking; which was just as well, as the effects of the dieselisation and the electrification work on the West Coast main line were just beginning to be felt. By the end of November, Nottingham shed had received an allocation of 'Royal Scots' – 46100 and 46157 – and we were soon seeing these through Leicester, as well as a smattering of other 'Scots', rare 'Jubilees', and the first visitations in any numbers by 'Patriots'. It was even harder to prize me away from the lineside! Unfortunately, I had not learnt much of the photographic skills needed – I still expected to be able to just point the camera and get results!

Another straw in the wind of progress was the arrival on 24 October 1959 at Leicester shed of an allocation of four diesel shunters – D3785-8. They caused great excitement and speculation, but no one seemed to sense what they presaged: the beginning of the end of steam. Seeing them standing in the shed yard, next to elderly D16 62612, was fascinating, if not a little incongruous. It was not long, though, with the advent of the 'Peaks', the 'Metrovicks' and other diesels which began to arrive, that we began to realise something of what was happening. Another sure sign was when station pilot 41268 – and old favourite which was kept immaculate by driver and fireman – was transferred away. These changes gave variety, but we did not particularly like them.

My first attempts with the new camera were on a dismal, misty day in February 1960. I was disappointed with the results, but I really was asking a lot of it. The extra scope of the negative size gave me confidence and I snapped away merrily on my first trip of the year to the sheds of the Manchester area, which thankfully, although the third week of February, was graced with reasonable weather. Starting at Rowsley and then Buxton, we visited, in turn, Stockport, Heaton Mersey, Trafford Park, Patricroft and Longsight – where I had my first sight of one of the new electrics, E3002.

But I was not consistent with the camera. In a two-month period in the early summer, I took a couple of shots at Rugby, on 6 May, ignored another trip there sixteen days later, snapped a K3 at Thurmaston on 7 June (on top of the last shot at Rugby, 45503 – ruining them both!), and then left my camera behind on a visit by rail to Crewe, which included a trip round the Works! What madness or weird logic possessed me, I know not. Fortunately, Les had taken his camera. By this time, Les Wade, David and I, had become the virtual Three Musketeers, meeting regularly and going everywhere together, mostly by bike. Les was the undoubted character among us, ever willing to 'have a go', but even he surpassed himself this day at Crewe, as he discovered the end of a finger, complete with nail, on the spiked railings surrounding North Shed yard! Presumably, some unfortunate had tried for a hasty escape and had misjudged things. Les found this fascinating, so much so that he prised the digit from the spike, wrapped it in his handkerchief and carried it home triumphant! Nothing could match that for the rest of that year, not even his attempts at chatting up a girl on the putting course in Ostend early in August, using his rather inadequate schoolboy French!

In retrospect, Derby Open Day on 27 August was interesting for, as I write this, Class 25s have not long become extinct on BR, and Class 45s are rapidly becoming so. On shed and Works that day, brand new, were D5132-40 and D11-19.

1. *Top left* I was almost on this train! It was the one that took me home from school every school-day for two years; the same engine and the same stock, but this picture was taken in the school holidays. 40146 pulls out of Loughborough station under the Great Central lines, at the head of the 5.20pm local to Leicester, August 1955. GEOFF KING

2. *Bottom left* Something of the feel and appeal of Rugby in those early days, showing the proliferation of semaphore signals and the amount of stock on view. 'Scot' 46106 *Gordon Highlander*, with straight-sided smoke deflectors, heads northwards on an express in May 1956, seen from an unusual vantage point.
GEOFF KING

3. *Above* One of those Specials that I missed! The sun comes from behind a cloud to illuminate 61665 *Leicester City* as she enters Belgrave & Birstall station, on the northbound *City of Leicester Holiday Express*, of 17 August 1956. Leicester Central shed had borrowed the engine for the week of these Holiday Expresses – a very nice touch by whoever had organised matters. GEOFF KING

4. *Top left* My first photo – with Dad's camera! I saw all the Garratts that were still extant when I started trainspotting and never tired of watching them. 47982 heads north from Syston North Junction, having just come off the Melton curve, with an empty iron-ore train on 1 June 1956. She was withdrawn six months later; but the semaphores lasted until 1987.

5. *Bottom left* The appeal of shed scenes – engines everywhere. Seen from the Birdcage, Leicester Midland (15C) houses 45267, 40452, 75059, 42373 and 44163, amongst others, on 4 June 1957. Thirty years later, the roundhouse area was home to a brand new power signal box and car park!

6. *Above* One of my earliest memories at Belgrave Road station, Leicester, known affectionately as the Great Northern, is of a J6 on a couple of coaches, to make up a workmen's (unadvertised) train. Here is just such a train – the 1.00pm (SO) to John O'Gaunt – seen entering Humberstone station, 6 October 1956. Note the delightful Northern somersault signal on the left.
GEOFF KING

7. *Above* A slightly unusual view of the seafront railway at Dawlish showing 4156 entering with a local from Exeter, July 1957.

8. *Top right* Another view of the sights of Derby Open Day, 30 August 1958; this time from my own primitive camera. Prototype diesel, 10000, stands amidst a lot of clutter, but is still the subject of much admiration.

9. *Bottom right* Although actually taken in 1961, this shot is symptomatic of what was seen at any time in those early days at Stratford shed – little tank engines, of all shapes and sizes. 68552 stands in the spring sunshine of 26 March, without connecting rods, although she had another seven months to live.
HUGH RAMSEY

ROLL THIS
WAY

10. *Top* Motive power for the trains to Rugby, was either
Stanier Class 3 2-6-2Ts (*see Plate 1*), Fowler Class 4 2-6-4Ts or,
as here, other 2-6-4Ts. I was pulled by 42541 to Rugby, but not
actually on this day, when she is seen at Wigston North Junction,
on the same day as Plate 11 below. The semaphore in the centre
now resides in a private garden! GEOFF KING

11. *Bottom* *The Thames-Clyde Express* was *the* prestigious
express, on the Midland main line and one that I saw every day
as it passed through Loughborough immediately before our
school train home. Booked to leave Leicester at 5.14pm,
Thursday, 18 June 1959, had 45568 *Western Australia* at the
head, with the unusual straight-sided tender, seen leaving
Knighton Tunnel. HORACE GAMBLE

12 & 13. Two views of the Central in Leicester.

Top GC 'Directors' were not uncommon visitors on locals from Nottingham, but were nonetheless a delight to see. 62661 *Gerard Powys Dewhurst* of Staveley (GC) shed, backs down to the turntable at the side of the station in the late afternoon sunshine on 13 June 1959. HORACE GAMBLE

Bottom The Central shed, down by the canal, was a long walk to reach, past hoards of often irritable fishermen but was well worth a visit – if you could avoid the foreman! In latter days, Midland engines mixed cheek-by-jowl with a variety of ER locos, as can be seen here: 42897 in company with 60887 (of York shed). Unusually, the 'Crab' was about to depart to haul the 5.46pm express to Manchester (ex-Marylebone), 13 August 1959. HORACE GAMBLE

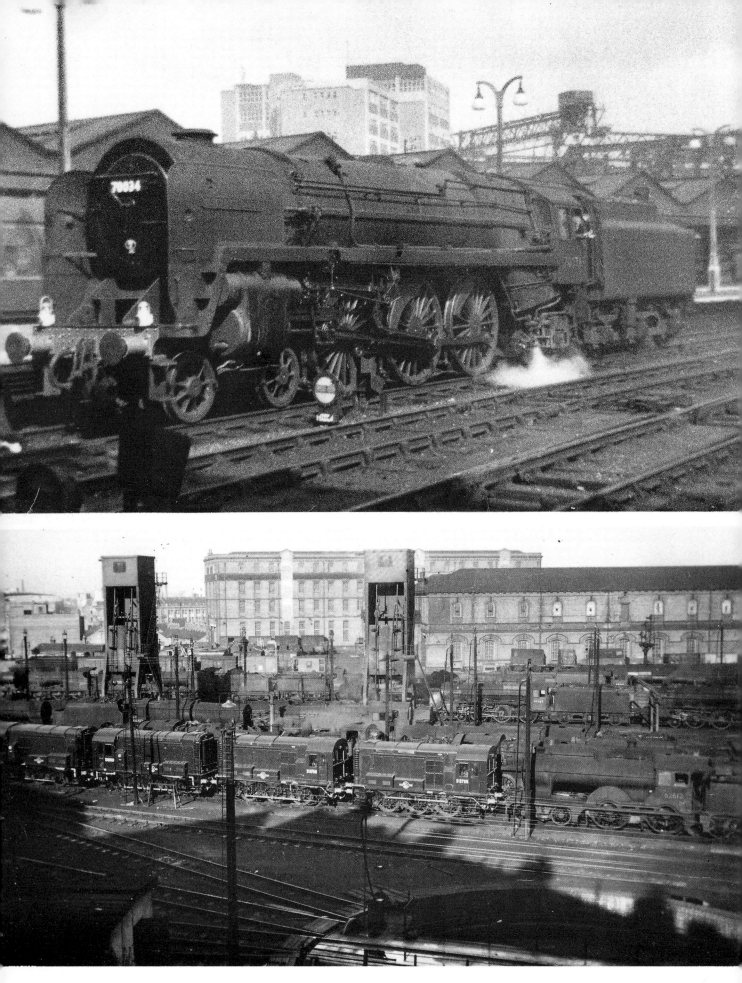

14. *Top* One of the delights of our trip to Liverpool Street, on 3 September 1959, was the sight of the ER 'Britannias'. 70034 *Thomas Hardy* backs out of the trainshed into the sunshine, having arrived with an express from Norwich.

15. *Bottom* 24 October 1959 was a momentous day in the history of Leicester Midland shed. Diesel shunters D3785-88 arrived, providing the hint of what was to come. On that first day, they stand in the yard, making interesting comparison with ER D16/3 62612; other companions include 44189, 44743 and 44984. LES WADE

16. *Top* I sat on this perch for hours, in the late '50s/early '60s, watching the trains go by, as Grandad had an allotment (which I later took over) immediately to the right of this view. The variety of trains was seemingly infinite and freight was common; here an immaculate K3, No. 61975, heads through Belgrave & Birstall station in the midday sunshine of 24 April 1957, evidencing some of the attraction. GEOFF KING

17. *Bottom* With the advent and expansion of electrification of the WCML, Classes were transferred to the Midland main line that hitherto had been much rarer. The 'Scots' were a case in point; here 46123 *Royal Irish Fusilier* saunters at a leisurely pace, southwards towards Leicester, through Thurmaston, with a rake of empty stock from Syston coach sidings, 11 April 1960.

18. *Above* One benefit of living near Leicester was the presence
of cross-country services, which often brought unusual or rare
motive power to the city. Both are encapsulated in one engine,
as 61657 *Doncaster Rovers* is seen leaving Syston station with the
1840 Leicester-Peterborough train, 13 April 1960. GEOFF KING

19. *Top right* In the heyday of steam, trip freights, shifting small
amounts of goods and vehicles locally from point to point, were
common. 43969 is in no hurry and the fireman has time to sit
back and enjoy the view, as the short rake ambles through
Thurmaston, southbound to Leicester, May 1960.

20. *Bottom right* On the Central, in Leicester, it was a regular
treat to see GW engines working in on the Bournemouth-York
services. They occasionally worked north, but usually came off
at Leicester before turning and preparing for the return trip. On
10 May 1960, 6976 *Graythwaite Hall* – a regular stands ready to
take the 1720 service to Woodford Halse. HORACE GAMBLE

21 & 22. Two views of a trip to Rugby, 22 May 1960.

Top 'Jubilee' 45705 *Seahorse* takes the avoiding line, on an up Special from Blackpool, bound for Euston.

Bottom Evidence of times to come, D313 draws close to the station from the south, on an unidentified express. Note the absence of yellow warning panel that would grace the front-end not too long afterwards.

23. *Top* As well as the trip freight seen in a previous photograph, the Midland main line saw many long-haul freights. 45120, with a good head of steam, takes a load southwards that originated in Carlisle, through Thurmaston, in August 1960.

24. *Bottom* Back at Rugby, on 16 August 1960, 44716 looks in highly creditable state, as she waits to enter the station area, on a train from Northampton.

25. *Top* One of the joys of visiting Grantham was the sight of A4s, especially if they were in full flight. 60026 *Miles Beevor* moves more slowly as she comes off shed and passes through the station, ready to take over an 'up' express to King's Cross, 19 August 1960.

26. *Bottom* I took a photograph on only one occasion from this bridge, but was graced with good fortune as I captured an 'Extra' Manchester-London express, diverted via the Midland main line due to electrification work on the WCML; a mixture of all sorts of coaches, including a Gresley vehicle up-front, and a view of 45596 *Bahamas*, rare to this line and with single chimney, seen leaving Syston on Sunday, 4 September 1960.

CHAPTER TWO

'961 was a momentous year.

I left school, started work (twice), had a thirteen-week holiday between the two jobs and, along the way, copped more engines in a seven-day period than ever before.

My first job was helping to build a sewage treatment plant at Wanlip, five miles or so to the north of Leicester. The weather that June seemed to be a mixture of either baking sunshine or rain. I was assigned, with a friend from school, to two Irish navvies who, on our first days, were 'digging out' one of the huge pipes that had already been sunk into the ground. It had been raining the few days before we started and the 'slurry' around the pipe was more water than soil! One of the Irishmen was at the foot of the pit, shovelling this stuff to his mate – who was at his shoulder level – who then shovelled it to me – at his shoulder level – and I shovelled it to John, my schoolmate, at my shoulder level. We were expected to keep pace with the men, who seemed never to stop, and the first day damn near killed me – 8am to 6pm, with only half-an-hour lunch, was most definitely not school hours! If I had stopped for long, I would have been buried in the mess being shovelled up to me and so had to keep going. I very quickly discovered blisters in abundance and muscles I never knew existed. I was not altogether sorry to be laid off after four weeks!

I travelled to this job by bike and we Three Musketeers (David, Les and myself), were now getting plenty of cycling practice, with regular trips to Rugby and Nuneaton. For our trip to Rugby on 15 April – a distance of 22 miles each way – Les had acquired an old army bike, with a fixed wheel and gearing. Whilst David and I notched down to low gear for the many hills, Les often had to stand up just to keep sufficient momentum, but then he would career down the slopes, standing on the fixed pedals, bobbing up and down like some demented fairground carousel. What onlookers must have thought of this, with the two of us laughing fit to burst behind, I cannot imagine! By this time, dieselisation was rapidly gaining ground on the WCML, with 50% of engines being non-steam on this day. Not liking diesels, Les and I invented a railway game, in biro, on the face of a handy poster by Rugby Station; it was a good game and we had plans of submitting it to Waddingtons, but somehow never got round to it.

My thirteen-week holiday began when I left the sewage farm, and it was to be a wonderful summer. The sun seemed always to be shining and the bridge, on the Midland main line at Thurmaston, became my second home, fortified midday with radish sandwiches! There I watched the influx of new 'Peak' diesels – a new one almost every day, it seemed, 23 May: D23 and D99; 25 May: D100; 26 May: D96; 27 May D102; and 4 June: D103 and D88.

The day before this, on 3 June, Brush Engineering at Loughborough held an Open Day. They were keen to show the latest techniques in engineering and the extent and range of their work, but we wanted to see the new diesels being built there. In various stages of construction were D0280 (later to emerge in lime green and chestnut brown as *Falcon* and became, via some osmosis, the prototype Class 47) and D5801-19 inclusive; and also on show was 10800, Built as part of British Railways' Modernisation Plan, for use on secondary duties, the latter had been withdrawn as early as July 1959, from Rugby shed, but had been re-acquired by Brush for use as a test bed.

At the same time, not far away, on the Central, we were being treated to another prototype, this time working. The Gas Turbine trial loco GT3 was allocated to Leicester to run the Marylebone trains and this it did, starting in May. Whilst a very handsome loco (and even acceptable, shaped as it was like a steam engine!), unfortunately it did not perform brilliantly and soon left.

Steam was now being withdrawn in even greater numbers, as the new motive power came on stream and both generations were to be seen at Derby one month later, on 2 July, where engines recalled for scrapping, were on shed and Works, cheek-by-jowl with new D36-D52. Strangely, though, two engines were tucked away in a woodyard, on the opposite side of the main lines to the Works. 43787 had been withdrawn in January 1959 from Warrington (Dallam) shed, and 41173 in February 1959 from Derby. Why they had escaped the cutter's torch in this way, or what later happened to them, I do not know. It is possible that they were once considered for preservation.

Whole services were now being taken over by diesels and a trip to Essendine on 7 August was timely, as this was the last summer that the non-stop King's Cross-Edinburgh *The Elizabethan*, was regularly steam hauled (*see Plate 34*). As from 1962, Deltics took over completely, although they were already in evidence, D9005 *The Prince of Wales's Own Regiment of Yorkshire* and D9007 *Pinza* being seen that day. Most trains, however, were still steam and in just a few hours of that afternoon we saw:

60014 *Silver Link* on the 'down' *Elizabethan*
60003 *Andrew K. McCosh* to Newcastle
60020 *Guillemot* on the 'up' *Flying Scotsman*
60049 *Galtee More* ex-Newcastle
60118 *Archibald Sturrock* to Leeds
D278 ex-Glasgow
60047 *Donovan* and 60841 on unidentified trains
D250 to Newcastle
60046 *Diamond Jubilee* ex-Newcastle
60054 *Prince of Wales* to Leeds
60524 *Herringbone* to Edinburgh
60024 *Kingfisher* on the 'up' *Elizabethan*
60125 *Scottish Union* ex-Leeds
60516 *Hycilla* to Hull
D9007 *Pinza* on the 'down' *Flying Scotsman*
60136 *Alcazar* ex-Hull
92140, 60061 *Pretty Polly*, 60124 *Kenilworth*, D348 and D284 on unidentified trains
60875 to Grantham
60034 *Lord Faringdon* to Glasgow
60148 *Aboyeur* to Leeds
60039 *Sandwich* on the 'up' *White Rose*
60108 *Gay Crusader* ex-York
60130 *Kestrel*, 60156 *Great Central*, D239 and 60908 on unidentified trains; all either enjoying the long slope down from Stoke Bank, or beginning to work hard up it!

Steam was also very much in evidence in Devon and Cornwall later in August, as The Three Musketeers descended on the area for their holiday based in Dawlish.

Having travelled from Leicester, via Birmingham, the Lickey Incline, Gloucester and Bristol, to reach Dawlish, we saw, happily, very few diesels; but the best was yet to come. We literally could not believe our eyes at the number and variety of trains/engines that rattled past our hotel at, seemingly, all hours of day and night. Our pens hardly paused, as we scribbled down the numbers and it was all we could do to tear ourselves away for our meals and bed! In the week 19-26 August we travelled extensively between Exeter/Exmouth Junction and Plymouth, and even ventured to the southernmost tip of the line at Penzance on 24 August. Because of financial constraints, I had to ration the photos, which irked me greatly in view of the opportunities – thirty years later, with 36 exposures and cheap films, I can only dwell on the shots I missed! In the seven days, I logged 651 engines (some more than once, admittedly) and of these, I copped 434, including a staggering 146 on the first day! But if I thought that was a lot, still more was to come.

Barely having regained breath after this jaunt, we travelled north to Scotland; but this time we had not booked anywhere, which led to interesting sleeping arrangements!

Travelling overnight (behind D87 to Leeds an then D13 to Carlisle), we saw little of the journey engines along it, as we fitfully tried to sleep. We arrived in Carlisle at the crack of dawn (or so seemed) and we set off, via bus and on foot, to 'do' th Carlisle sheds, starting at Upperby. Nothing excitement here, but Canal shed was much bette housing engines foreign to us southerners. I was ju getting into the swing of recording highlights on filr when my camera jammed and no amount of gentl persuasion had any effect! The very first mornin virtually five minutes from the station, and I wa without a camera! (And I was not able to get it fixe until our return to Leicester.)

Having visited Kingmoor, we then caught the trai to Glasgow – via the G&SW route, to St Enoch. B the time we reached the station, it was getting late, s having had a snack in the buffet, we lay down o platform benches to attempt sleep. Hardly had w become horizontal than a porter demanded what th hell we were doing! Having explained our plight, h must have taken pity on us as, carefully checking tha superiors were not watching, he informed us that th rake of carriages in the nearby platform was not due t leave until 7am the next morning and, if we wanted we could spend the night in them – providing we wer out by that time! We jumped at the chance. Bein non-corridor, we decided that we would all share th same compartment – which meant one of us sleepin on the luggage rack, while the other two had the seats Poor old Les – the iron stanchions supporting the rac were not at all comfortable and the string of the rac itself certainly left its impression!

Fitfully rested and then having made a brav attempt at a wash-and-brush-up in the Gents Toilet(!) we set off next morning to bash the Glasgov sheds and Works – and a most successful day it wa visiting Eastfield, Cowlairs Works, St Rollox Work and shed, Polmadie, Corkerhill, before returning t the city, to catch a train to Edinburgh (and all this b foot and bus!).

We reached the capital city exhausted – and, again nowhere to sleep! This time we plumped for the Men' Waiting Room and settled down – me on a bench David on the table and Les on a chair by the table. slept like a log, but Les was disturbed by the Railwa Police, curious as to who he was, what he was doin and why he was there; and David woke on on occasion, to meet the bleary stare of a bushy-bearde sailor, his head on the table next to David's Somewhat stiff and unkempt by now, we spent th following day travelling to Thornton Junction Haymarket, Dalry Road and St Margarets, befor catching a train back south. Somehow we did thi comfortably and it was still daylight as we headed fo York. We were hauled by A4 60034 *Lord Faringdor* and Les wanted to put his head out of the window to see what was coming the other way. As the engine wa pushing out all manner of muck, he first put out hi hand as a trial and immediately let out a squeal o pain, as a red-hot cinder burned into his palm. We were very careful after that!

In those three short days this trio of, by now, ragged

nd dirty schoolboys had seen over 900 different ngines and I had copped 767; and a highlight, which ow, so many years and events later seems quite ncredible, was the sight of 114 engines on Polmadie hed. Spotters of the 1980s do not know what they ave missed.

One could be excused for thinking that we would be atiated by these trips and take a break from spotting or a while – no such thing. We were quickly back at ld haunts, like Grantham and Rugby and then, on 17 eptember, I joined the AMR charter train, the *Don-'or-Dar Flyer* – visiting, not surprisingly, Doncaster, 'ork and Darlington – to be hauled by restored Midland 'Compound' 1000. This was a magic trip vith, again bewildering varieties of motive power – team and diesel – and highlights such as WCML lectrics being built, D5578 in experimental blue very, and several Departmentals.

The following Saturday saw me in Birmingham – ot primarily for trains this time; I went for a elevision screen test! Those old enough to emember ITV's pop show, 'Thank Your Lucky tars', will recall the panel of teenagers each week iving their verdicts on new records. I went to test for his along with others, where we sat on high stools, nder hot lights in front of TV cameras, feeling like rize idiots. I was the last in the row and everyone had xpressed my thoughts by the time my turn came. 'herefore, somewhat at a loss for something new to ay, I failed to meet the standards. I did not see her nere, but just a few weeks later, the infamous Janice ppeared on the programme, with her Brummy 'Oi'll ive it foive' immediately becoming a nationwide atchphrase.

Up to this time I had travelled with other clubs to arious parts of the country but, increasingly, I was ecoming frustrated at them not visiting the sheds I vanted to go to. There was only one thing to do, to tart my own club – the Thurmaston Railway Society vas born.

Our first trip was a quite moderate affair, with a roup of us going to March and New England sheds. 'his was successful and those with me wanted more – ne die was cast. But first came work!

I was due to start work with Barclays Bank on 16)ctober, but I had booked a trip to Blackpool lluminations for the following Saturday and so, earing in mind that all Banks opened on Saturdays in hose days, I rather cheekily said I would start on the ollowing Monday, 23 October. Incredibly, they greed – and off to Blackpool I went, with David, Les nd one or two others. We did Blackpool shed while /e were there – in the dark, when there seemed to be ngines everywhere, waiting to take their return xcursions. But as well as the Illuminations, there was nother call on our attentions. Girls somehow seemed o becoming increasingly attractive; could it be there vas something else besides trainspotting?!

Starting work had three immediate advantages – I ad money; I was working in the centre of Leicester nd, thus, could easily walk up to the Birdcage at unchtimes; and there were more girls, both staff and ustomers. Working girls seemed so much more grown up and attractive than those at school, although those who were my immediate superiors certainly did not make my life easy!

I quickly began daily trips to the Birdcage and soon went even further, daring to venture into the shed buildings – which, without a permit, was dangerous. After a few weeks, I approached the shed foreman for permission to visit daily. Having looked me up and and down, he obviously thought (in my Barclays suit!) that I was worth trusting and gave me the go-ahead. This arrangement worked wonders for a few months, until one day I literally bumped into an Inspector. He was not amused at that or my permission and the latter was rescinded; I was back to bunking the shed, furtively!

There was one other who made regular trips to the Birdcage; we got to talking, became friends, played tennis, he joined the Ten-Pin Bowling team which I captained, and when later he got married, I was his Best Man. Peter thus joined The Three Musketeers and we became The Gang Of Four!

1962 carried on where 1961 had left off, with trips seemingly every week to all points of the compass, either under the Thurmaston Railway Society (TRS) banner or solo, and I took every opportunity to further the habit. By the end of 1961, after only six years of spotting, I had seen 8,579 different engines; I knew there were still many more thousands to go and was still determined to try to see them all. Thus it was that when I was sent to Wimbledon by the Bank for a fortnight's course, as well as scribbling every number I could each day, as I travelled by train to and from Wimbledon station, I stayed in London over the middle weekend and did as many sheds as possible, visiting, along the way, Norwood Junction shed for the one and only time. Others have said that when they are sat on a river bank, with rod and line in front of them, they are at peace with the world. I was in like state that weekend. I travelled from shed to shed, literally on Cloud Nine, totally relaxed and happy – almost regardless and oblivious of what engines were actually there. That feeling confirmed for me that trainspotting was in my blood and it is a feeling that is still there, just as strongly, twenty-five years later.

Also, the camera bug was biting harder at this time and I began logging the exposures to judge against the printed result. Dad having been a photographer in the RAF during the War, he was able to give me valuable tips, to the extent that I was very pleased with most of my 'judged' exposures – all done without the aid of a light meter. Unfortunately, I began to get cocky and decry all those who used such 'artificial' aids. When I changed cameras a year or so later, I was undone and now I wish I had been a little more humble and used the instrument to give me better pictures. Also my self-confidence was beginning to tell on the TRS.

On 1 July we set off with a coachload of members – average age around 13-14 – for the south. It was a bright, sunny day and I aimed to cover as much ground as possible (even having two bus drivers to cover the day's driving). We started at Bristol (Barrow Road) shed; then went to St Philip's Marsh, Bath Road, Bath (Green Park), Salisbury, Swindon

Museum (but neither Works nor shed as my persuasive powers failed me!), Didcot, Oxford and Banbury. In those days before motorways this was, at best, a long haul and with shed visits, etc, it was past 10pm when we fetched up at Banbury. The foreman was not pleased when he found us three-quarters round the shed and we were summarily dismissed; I did not mind, though, as it had been a super day and we were on our way home. Unfortunately, the members' parents were not so calm and, wondering where on earth we were, they caused Dad's phone to become red hot, as they called and re-called for news. When I eventually got home, at past midnight, I was very quickly red hot too! I was glad to be going on holiday the following Saturday.

As in 1961, Les, David and I trekked north to Scotland, but this time we had booked a week's base in Perth; no more sleeping on stations – Dad's orders!

There were changes, obviously, to the previous year but, thankfully, dieselisation was not yet all-conquering and electrification for the area was still just a dream; thus we enjoyed 46134 *The Cheshire Regiment* and 45029 double-heading us to Glasgow, having quickly done the Carlisle sheds. As we travelled north, it was nice to see old veterans still around, such as 54507 at Beattock (although in store) and we relished the thought of what might be lurking in corners further on. In the days that followed, we visited Perth shed every day and were amazed at the number of changes daily, as well as radiating to Aberdeen, Dundee/Thornton Junction, Grangemouth/Bo'ness Docks, Edinburgh and even back to Glasgow for a day. Bo'ness was a sad sight, with lines of stored, forlorn engines – not, unfortunately, in a position or weather to photograph.

Each day would see us back at Perth, rounding off at the local (large) Transport Cafe, for our evening meal. The women behind the counter were marvellous – after only the second day, we did not have to order. They saw us in the queue and merely asked, 'The usual?'

14 July was a sad day. Not only were we returning home, but we were leaving behind many locos that we knew we would never see again. Some had still been in steam, such as 54463 – the last of her class – but so many others had been in store, and nearly every shed we had visited had had engines with sacks over their chimneys, and some even had already reached the stage of running out of sacking, engines being merely dumped in side roads. The tragic waste of steam was gathering pace.

As well as TRS trips, there were still AMR outings, on one of which, to Leeds on 29 July, we had half-an-hour to kill in the centre of the city. One of our number went out, determined, and came back with a girl on each arm. What his secret was I do not know, but they were in tears when our coach left! There were trips to favourite haunts and Derby Open Day. The virgin territories yielded new delights, but the tried and tested areas began to have less appeal and to have to highlight such as DP2 at Rugby on 11 August, an 'Patriots' in store there on 20 July, was sad indeed.

The TRS trip to Swindon, Basingstoke and Reading on 2 September was much better. Despite the increasing number of diesels on the Western region, Swindon shed was almost exclusively steam and, on Works, although D1009-23 were in the process of construction, there were still many, many steam engines being repaired; Basingstoke had a healthy complement; Reading (WR) was again almost exclusively steam and the Southern shed was still open, with nine engines on show, including 30496.

A TRS trip to Manchester two weeks later also found much steam in evidence, including the delightfully diminutive 51204, 51232 and 51237 at Agecroft and 94 out of 100 steam at Gorton (although many of these in store). And a fortnight after that, a trip to the Crewe/Chester areas showed again there was much steam about. But these were 'false' times as the spread of dieselisation and electrification was unstoppable, and the signs were made even clearer during the TRS trip to the Doncaster/Sheffield area on 28 October where, on Staveley (GC) shed, 29 out of the 54 on view were in store, including 18 B1s, 'Jubilees' and 2 'Scots'.

Railwaywise, one of the later trips of the year was made, in the company of Peter, on a Derbyshire Railway Society (DRS) two-day trip to Carlisle via the Leeds area sheds, working back along the Cumbrian Coast and the North-West sheds, as far south as Warrington. Although new sheds were visited – most notably, Workington and Barrow, normally well out of my scope – the most memorable point came on our arrival at Wigan (L&Y) shed, code 27D. Happily, 2 of the 32 engines on shed were in steam, but unhappily, there seemed to be some defect in the shed's ventilation, as all this steam and other emissions were not escaping, resulting in a thick green fug that hung down to just about head height. It was physically difficult to see the numbers on the cab sides through the fog, and all of us came out of the shed building coughing and spluttering, eyes streaming. The life expectancy of railmen there must have been in weeks!

Numerically, the year had been my best yet, with no fewer than 3,198 cops; but this was deceptive and would not be repeated. But the year did end on one very positive note for me. On our drive round the Sheffield District, we were listening to Alan Freeman's Sunday pop programme (on the Light Programme) and heard the first play of Duane Eddy's '(Dance With The) Guitar Man'. Within a fortnight, it was in the charts and at the turn of the year was in the Top Ten. As a fervent fan of Duane Eddy, I was delighted.

27. *Above* In 1961 Leicester City reached the FA Cup Final (for the first time since 1949 and only the second time in their history). There were many Specials for the event on 6 May and the Central was host to a good number, being so convenient for Wembley. Here a First Class only Excursion to Wembley Hill passes Leicester South Goods, behind 45532 *Illustrious* of Nottingham (16A) shed, on the outward journey. Sadly City lost! HORACE GAMBLE

28. *Left* Fifteen days after the above, on 21 May 1961, the aesthetically very pleasing GT3 stands under the sheer legs of Leicester Central shed. Present on the Central for only a matter of weeks, she was on trial with a twice daily run to Marylebone, having arrived direct from an exhibition at Marylebone on 16 May, and her light brown livery was a delightful variation of colour.

29, 30 & 31. A trio of diesels on show at Brush Open Day, 3 June 1961.

Top left As can be seen from the notice strung on the engine-front, there were intended to be 226 of these Type 2s, but the actual number built (of what was to become Class 31) was 263, such was their success. By her destination blinds, she is advertising on the side!

Top right The prototype (and ultimately the only one of its kind), D0280 stands nearing completion, in primer, in the workshops. Eventually to carry the name *Falcon* after the Brush Works, it worked mostly on the Western Region of BR, but was not an unmitigated success, with much of its potential being lost to overtaking events.

Bottom left Having been a creature of the Modernisation Plan for locals and branch line work, 10800 had already been withdrawn in July 1959. Brush Engineering at Loughborough took her back and restored her for their own use; she looks handsome here, proudly on display.

32. *Above* The date is Sunday, 18 June 1961 and *Peak* D105 is still new. She takes up a lot of room in Leicester shed yard and she and her sisters would displace much steam before they were done! Also in the picture are: 43861, 44156, D3786, 44519, 43937 and 58137; the latter providing a nice contrast. LES WADE

33. *Top left* Midland 4F 0-6-0s were extremely well-travelled engines and they turned up on all sorts of duties. 44173 has a healthy load behind her as she enters Syston station at the head of a Yarmouth (Beach)-Leicester train. Though taken on a bright, sunny 11 August 1956, this view was quite common on this line well into the Sixties. GEOFF KING

34. *Bottom left* The afternoon David and I spent at Essendine was magic. To see A4s, A3s, etc, at speed, storming the bank in both directions, was exhilarating; but not quite so easy to capture on film! 1961 was the last year of steam on the non-stop *Elizabethan* express, handled to the end by A4s. 60024 *Kingfisher* literally races downhill, towards London, 7 August.

35. *Above* Virtually everything that can be seen in this view, including the bridge from which the photo is taken, has been obliterated. The station area is now a toy store; the warehouse on the right, a Sainsbury's hypermarket; and where the engine is has now become a housing estate. 61285 looks defiant, however, as she makes a spirited exit from Leicester, Belgrave Road station, on a train to Skegness, August 1961. GEOFF KING

36. *Top* Another way of reaching Rugby from Leicester was by way of the Central. The 12.35 train is about to leave, behind 42556, on Saturday, 28 October 1961. HORACE GAMBLE

37. *Above* One of the joys of the Devon holiday in 1961 was seeing engines that never strayed far from their home depot. A case in point is 1363, seen between duties on Laira shed, 22 August.

38. *Top* Evoking fond memories of the smoky atmosphere which often hung around steam sheds, 92054 backs further into the Leicester Midland shed yard after taking water, 13 September 1961. LES WADE

39. *Above* A sight that, technically, is possible of closely re-creating, following the reopening in 1987, 'Castle' 7036 *Taunton Castle* enters Birmingham (Snow Hill) station with a Paddington-Birkenhead service, 28 September 1961.

40 & 41. Two views of B1s.

Top 61299 waits patiently, as passengers board the 12.00 service to Woodford Halse at Leicester Central, 28 October 1961.
HORACE GAMBLE

Bottom One of the few named B1s, 61379 *Mayflower* stands in august company with 70035 *Rudyard Kipling* on Immingham shed, 27 May 1962.

42 & 43. Two views of the Scottish holiday of 1962.

Top Corkerhill shed was always a delight to visit, with its wide mix of engine types and its sprinkling of 'namers'. 'Jubilee' 45693 *Agamemnon* stands in the summer sun of 10 July.

Bottom Bathgate was home at this time to many stored 'old-timers', not least of which was 62685 *Malcolm Graeme*, having been a stationary boiler and with some strange mixture on buffer and front wheel! 12 July.

44. *Top* Visits to Rugby by 1962 were nowhere near as interesting, steamwise, as previously, but Specials did still bring in the odd engine. 45417 coasts into the station from the north with an unidentified excursion, 16 August.

45. *Bottom* The Leicester-Swannington line, one of *the* oldest in the country, was ever a delight right to the end. Due to the Glenfield Tunnel, engines had to be of limited dimensions, which meant small engines of venerable vintage in the main. 58148, marshalling brake vans, for a run to the Leicester (West Bridge) terminus, was a regular star, 8 September 1962. GEOFF KIN

46. *Top* Of all my railway trips, shed visits were my favourites, with the ability of getting close to the engines. 44566 looks well cared for, Trafford Park, 16 September 1962.

47. *Bottom* A delightful shed to visit was Crewe (Gresty Lane), sub to North shed and home to the GW engines that reached the town. The MR is portrayed, however, in this view of 41241 (now preserved), 30 September 1962.

48. *Top* Sunday, 28 October 1962 was a dismal day to go shed-bashing, but A3 60109 *Hermit* looks fine under ominous clouds in Doncaster Works. LES WADE

49. *Bottom* Same venue, but a different view! 42527 will not see any more service, as the tanks are all that is left after the cutters' torch! LES WADE

50. *Top* Although still bearing their BR numbers, J50s 68911 (*left*) and 68914 were withdrawn from full stock in 1960. They are here in service as Departmentals at Doncaster Works as, respectively, Nos 10 and 11. They lasted in this guise until 1965, but are seen here temporarily resting, 28 October 1962. LES WADE

51. *Bottom* Very much alive, and casting a smoky haze over the view of the shed, is 61249 *FitzHerbert Wright*, negotiating the points at the entrance to Sheffield (Darnall) shed, 28 October 1962. LES WADE

52. *Top* Still in sight of her working companions, 64373 will not, however, turn a wheel again in revenue-earning effort as she has just been withdrawn. Darnall shed, 28 October 1962. LES WADE

53. *Bottom* I had to gain entrance to Wolverhampton (Stafford Road) shed by the back way on this day and this scene did nothing to cheer me up. In store stripped of their numbers and names, and never to work again for BR are: (*left to right*) 6017 *King Edward IV*, 6012 *King Edward VI*, 6014 *King Henry VII*, 6015 *King Richard III*, and 6022 *King Edward III*, 1 December 1962.

CHAPTER THREE

1963 was the year of the big snows and right in the middle of it – 16-17 February – I had arranged a two-day mini-bus trip to Newcastle!

Earlier in the month I had made a solo trip round London (again courtesy of a Barclays Bank course) – picking up a 'guest' at King's Cross, who was only too pleased to get the chance of visiting various sheds, including Stratford – and that wasn't too bad, but snow fell steadily during the month, and the seven days before the Newcastle trip there was much deliberation, heart-searching and weather-forecast-watching, as both bus company and I tried to assess the trip's viability. In the end, the company was prepared to take a chance and I certainly was! So, *very* early on Saturday morning, wrapped up to the eyeballs and equipped with War Rations (!), we headed north. The main part of the journey was via the A1, then a mere dual-carriageway for part of the way but with one carriageway blocked by snow and on all sides drifts up to 8ft. However, we safely made Darlington Works – much to the astonishment of the Works Manager when he saw where we had come from – and then we proceeded to Thornaby and West Hartlepool before retiring for the night. The driver, Les and I slept in a hotel in Consett, whereas the others were billeted at a youth hostel, a few miles away. Having dropped them at the hostel, we looked anxiously at the snow around us (and at the angry looking sky) as we drove to Consett. That night it snowed some more and we woke to brilliant sunshine; but having breakfasted, we could not find the mini-bus! Where we had parked it, there was only a 7ft mound of snow! It took some digging to actually discover it but, remarkably, it started first time and we were able to head to the hostel only an hour or so behind time. The trip there was uneventful, in the sunshine, but the hostel was at the foot of a steep hill, just passable by one vehicle (either way) at a time. Having turned round, we made a run at the hill and were going well when, suddenly, we saw a snowplough coming down the hill, pushing walls of snow before it. We were forced to slow and, not surprisingly, lost our grip on the road. No amount of bouncing and pushing by the eleven intrepid spotters, could grip the road or hold the bus and it slid all the way back down the hill. The snowplough driver did not understand our cursing and gesticulations as he passed us at the bottom of the hill; I am sure he

thought that he had done us a good turn! After another run at the hill, we eventually made the top – after a little more sliding, bouncing and pushing – but we had lost another hour or so.

We determined to complete as much as possible and set off for Blaydon, where we saw more disheartening sights – 32 out of 57 in store, including 60521 *Watling Street*, 60076 *Galopin*, 60517 *Ocean Swell*, 60539 *Bronzino*, 60511 *Airborne*, 60072 *Sunstar*, 60538 *Velocity*, 60079 *Bayardo* and 60501 *Cock o' the North*. During the rest of the day, we managed Gateshead, Blyth (North and South – and boy, was it cold on the ferry between them!), Percy Main, Heaton, Tyne Dock and Sunderland. Although the number tally was most acceptable – with 394 cops over the two days – the sight of so many engines in store was dispiriting, especially as so many of them obviously had years of work left in them.

Considering the time that we had had snow – from memory, it had started on Boxing Day – when the thaw came, it disappeared incredibly quickly. Thus, when we went on our next trip, to Leeds on 3 March, the sun shone brightly and all traces of the snow had gone. But the stored mania had not and engines began appearing at unexpected locations, such as 46117 *Welsh Guardsman*, 46109 *Royal Engineer*, 46161 *King's Own* and 46113 *Cameronian* out of commission on Neville Hill, that day, still very much an E.R. shed.

TRS was now in full swing and I began looking around for fresh fields to visit. On 30 March we travelled to the Hull/York area and during the day visited Goole. Having trudged what seemed miles to actually reach the shed yard, we were greeted by the foreman, at the head of the yard, with a very stern look on his face and his arms folded. He looked an immovable obstacle and we quickly learned the reason. He pointed to D6733 in the yard and it was quietly smouldering. The day before, some unknown 'enthusiasts' had set fire to the loco and had very nearly caused serious injury and damage. Needless to say, he was not kindly disposed towards trainspotters! He did, however, after some coaxing, allow Les to photo the scene and one other to collect the numbers of the locos visible from the yard. (*see Plate 59*)

On 21 April we went to a corner of the North-West previously unvisited, starting with Horwich Works. Apart from seeing builders plates on engines, I knew little of the place and was fascinated to see it at work, with 11324 and 11305 busy shunting engines around the yards. Never a glamorous place, unlike Crewe, Doncaster or Swindon, the complement was all workaday locos, either freight or secondary passenger; but as well as the two engines above, it was interesting to see the likes of 52515 and 51207 and fascinating to see the delightful narrow gauge Works engine, *Wren*.

Virgin territory such as this, though, was becoming harder and harder to find and most of the time we were forced to revisit old haunts; but these still produced the odd gem – even occasionally in non-railway terms, such as the sight of 64875 stored at the back of Woodford Halse shed, on 28 April, with the legend 'DUANE EDDY' scrawled across its boiler door, in chalk letters a foot high! And it was nothing to do with me!

One spin-off of all this travel was that there were now quite a few classes of engine, of which I only needed to see one or two, to clear the lot. Of the 'Jubilees', I needed to see just one – 45719 *Glorious*. I had heard rumour that it was stored on Bank Hall shed in Liverpool. I resolved to try and see it and so promptly caught a train at Leicester, bound for Liverpool, without any permits and no real idea of what I would do when I reached my destination.

Once in the city, I headed straight for Bank Hall depot, but the shed entrance was off Stanley Road, opposite the station. Unfortunately, it led straight into a passage, with the foreman's office on the righthand side. My first attempt – a courteous request for permission – was met by a very flat 'NO!'. Emerging back into the light, I ran into a railman who immediately guessed my plight. He offered to engage the foreman, while I crept through behind his coat-tails; he played his part and I crouch-walked past the office window, Red Indian-style, to reach the stairs that would take me down into the shed itself. Going down the rows of engines, I could not see any 'Jubilee' at all, until I came across 45657 *Tyrwhitt*, and 45698 *Mars*. With just one row to go, I was despairing, but there, at the very back, the last engine on the road, was my goal – I had cleared my 'Jubilees'. I stifled a cheer, but did a private leap-kick to celebrate; having gazed on her for a few moments, I then made my way back to the stairs. Overjoyed and internally bubbling with happiness, I still did not want to run into the foreman, and opened the door in some trepidation; my luck held and I made for the street door and safety. A voice called out behind me, but I was not about to stop! Less than a fortnight later, I brought the TRS to Bank Hall, on a Liverpool area trip, (this time with a permit) – all three 'Jubilees' had vanished. I had completed the class by the skin of my teeth!

On the latter trip, we again broke new ground, travelling through the Mersey Tunnel to Birkenhead. Although the trip was a success numberwise, the bus company did not appreciate the local kids hurling half-house bricks at us as we drove away!

One aspect of running TRS, always to mind, was control. Making sure the members behaved themselves, when visiting sheds, trying to prevent petty theft (like the two new members trying to

dislodge shed plates at Woodford Halse!) and above all, keeping a constant head count. I did slip up, though, on 9 June, when visiting Lees (Oldham) shed. Having done the shed, we all piled back into the coach, anxious to be off to the next depot. It was not until we were a couple or so miles down the road that someone noticed that 'Chirp' (one of our older members) was missing. Retracing our route, we found him resolutely striding out, about half-a-mile from the shed. Somehow we had left him behind, but where he thought he was walking to, I am not sure!

As well as these trips, I was keeping up my daily visit to the local railway, but the lunchtime routine had changed slightly, as now Les, Peter and I met in the Buffet of Leicester Central Station. Not only was the Double Diamond refreshing, but the parade of engines was frequent and varied; but on 25 May we had an unusual treat, seeing D6815, D6816, D6798, 92229 and 92244 heading south in convoy. Where they were bound, or where they had been, I never did find out.

1963's summer holiday was taken early, in June, when I was joined by a new friend, Keith, for two weeks in South Wales, based at a guest house in Barry. Limited a little by the sheer logistics of rail travel, we did, nevertheless, travel extensively, covering places like Swansea, Port Talbot, Severn Tunnel Junction, Cardiff, Pontypool Road, Aberbeeg, Abercynon (which I was pronouncing wrongly, until corrected by a DMU driver), Merthyr, Danygraig, Neath, Tondu (which, for no accountable reason, I fell in love with), Treherbert, Hereford, Craven Arms, Neyland (which we just managed to do, by bus, from Milford Haven, getting back in time to make our connection), Carmarthen and Llanelly. But, undoubtedly the highlight of the week was our first sight of Barry Docks and the engines bought by Dai Woodham. Still early days in his now legendary stockpiling of engines, we were open-mouthed to see: 5182, 5547, 9445, 9449, 9499, 7723, 5422, 9491, 8419, 5510, 9462, 5558, 7722, 9468, 5794, 5557, 5552, 5553, 5542, 5538, 5572, 5539, 4566, 5521, 4561, 5193, 4588, 5532, 5526, 6023, 6024, 5541, 4270, and 4253; and I was even more amazed to see, on the smokebox door of 6023, 'DUANE EDDY'! The chalk fiend had struck again! (I would still like to know who it was.) I would see these engines many more times, over the next few years, together with many more additions, but the strength of the visual impact was never quite the same as that first time. I literally could not believe my eyes (nor, in a sense, did I want to).

Back home in Leicester all manner of interesting locos were being seen, displaced from the West Coast main line, by the twin elements of dieselisation and electrification, but I was spending much less time by the lineside now, as I had bought a car. My pride and joy was a 1956 Ford Popular, a sit-up-and-beg vehicle, with a 6-volt battery, three gears, windscreen wipers that worked off the engine's air system (and no washers) and a wooden floor. It cost me £100 and certainly made travelling to sheds so much easier, and many other places accessible that would otherwise have been impossible to reach. Also it was to prove useful in my social life with the girls who were still trying to distract me from the iron road; one in particular was soon to enter my life.

One of my first outings in the car was a solo trip to March and New England. It was sad to see engines of the calibre of A3s, A1s, V2s and even 'Britannias' in store (70030 *William Wordsworth*, 70013 *Oliver Cromwell* and 70002 *Geoffrey Chaucer*, at March), but the freedom afforded by the car – on roads still quite empty – just added to that peace which I felt when with railways.

On 21 October Barclays Bank saw fit to transfer me to Syston, four miles to the north of Leicester. There were just five of us on the staff, one was a young girl called Gill; I did not know it at the time, but we were to become much closer than mere workmates.

The day before this transfer, TRS had revisited Banbury, Swindon, Didcot and Reading (including the Southern shed, still at that time a depot in its own right) and it was gratifying to see the number of steam still being repaired on Works, despite the spread of diesels and the storage of other steam on the depots. Also gratifying at this time was a two-day trip, again with Peter and the DRS, to an area encompassed by Eastleigh, Exmouth Junction, Laira, Okehampton, Barnstaple, Taunton, Yeovil and Westbury. Not only was it again breaking new ground, but there was a satisfying lack of diesels, with the sole exception of Laira, where 31 of 34 working engines were non-steam.

Numberwise, 1963 had again been a good year – although needing much more effort, travelling and money – with 2,768 cops in the year bringing my grand tally to 14,545, of which 11,666 were steam!

Visiting so many places, I had long felt that I was too restricted by 12-exposure black-and-white film. 36-exposure 35mm slides looked far more attractive, with the added advantage of colour. I dropped hints like bombs in the lead-up to Christmas and my parents proved they were not totally deaf – I was given a new Minolta SLR. I could not wait to try it out; but the only thing I was interested in taking was railways and, therefore, I had to wait for the DRS trip to Manchester, on 9 February 1964. Regrettably, the weather was appalling and my pig-headedness over exposure guesswork did not help! Neither did the Kodak film, which I found far too blue. I quickly switched allegiance to Agfa and was far more satisfied. The extra exposures gave me much more freedom and I became far more 'snap happy'; but still I was not learning much about framing and picture composition – in retrospect, too many photos have poles sticking out of the top of boilers, etc, and too many have 'edges' chopped off. But the results *were* teaching me lessons; I was continually disappointed and gradually improved over the years.

By this time, in the wake of the disastrous Beeching Axe, there was so much that was disappearing. Not just steam engines now, but whole lines and there was a succession of 'last trains'. Inexplicably, I showed no interest in recording these, contenting myself with the shed visits, also involving myself further in things non-railway. Being an active member of the Thurmaston

Methodist Church, I gravitated to the drama group and this, plus those girls, were taking more of my time and interest. I fought this tendency hard, though, and purposely went off on occasion on my own, to find railways. Thus it was, that I tracked down the rumoured 600 Group scrap yard, in the depths of the countryside, near Kettering. On a sunny 24 May, I took David and Les, to show them the sights – various items partly cut, including some Underground stock, plus 5018 *St Mawes Castle*, 30507, 30921 *Shrewsbury*, 30935 *Sevenoaks*, 31922 and the remains of 33024. After that visit it was a regular pilgrimage, to keep up to date and watch the changing pattern of locos through 600 Group's hands. Such was the now mass slaughter of engines that BR could not keep pace in their own Works and they were forced to use outside contract cutters, who bid against each other for this scrap source and many handled large quantities of locos over the next few years.

With the development of modernisation, steam was being eradicated from ever-increasing pockets throughout the country. I knew now that I could not fulfil my original ambition of seeing all the engines, but I was still determined to capture as many as possible. I began looking at areas where there were still things for me to find and, thus, I purposely visited Staveley, on 14 June, to see the small Johnson tanks, while they were still at work; I saw only two, however, 41528 and 41734. Fratton was next on the list, in a trip on 21 June, to see the locos housed for preservation – 120, 30926 *Repton*, 30245, 30925 *Cheltenham*, 30850 *Lord Nelson* and 30777 *Sir Lamiel* – plus others also in store, but destined not to survive.

In all my junketings over the country, there was one area that had so far eluded me – the South-East. I determined to try and correct this and on Sunday 19 July, as TRS, we visited Guildford, Redhill and Feltham, before turning back north, via some London sheds. Not as far as I would have liked to go, but, despite some urging from the members to venture as far as Ashford and the surrounding area, I had been given strict instructions from the relevant parents that there must be no repeats of those previous late returns! If I wanted the Club to survive, I had to take heed. The trip was successful, however, and the visit to Redhill especially so, noting the presence of ER B1 61313, which had failed on some working, the nature of which I could not establish; and the remains of 31797, at the back of the shed. It was only twenty-eight days earlier that I had photographed it, intact, at Eastleigh!

But the week before all this, I had participated in a most enjoyable railtour organised by DRS and which took A1 60114 *W.P. Allen* to Worcester (for the one and only time?). The trip was memorable in many ways: we had excellent weather after many days of rain; we worked wrong line down the Lickey Incline, due to engineering works; we had a spirited run behind 5054 *Earl of Ducie*; and had the privilege of arriving at Worcester, Hereford, Pontypool Road, Cardiff and Severn Tunnel Junction stations, to be ferried by a whole series of coaches to the sheds. The organisation was superb but, unfortunately, the A1 failed at Worcester and could not haul us back to Derby.

For our holiday in 1964, the Gang of Four had chosen to return to Scotland, only this time we would travel around by road, and would include places we had previously been unable to get to – like Dumfries, Stranraer, Ayr, Carstairs and Stirling.

The first part of the journey was by rail, with the car being loaded late one Friday night, 21 August, at Nottingham station, to be part of our Midnight Express for Carlisle! Trusting to BR's organisation, we boarded the train and I slept somewhat apprehensively as we sped north, over the Settle & Carlisle (then just another route), to arrive at Carlisle at 6am. To our relief, the car was with us, but it took the shunter an hour to put the van into the appropriate siding and for us to retrieve it! Sadly, the Nottingham men had not fixed the restraining bars properly inside the van, with a resultant dent in the wing, caused by the car shifting with the train's movement. A good start to our holiday (and one which would be argued over with BR for several months to come)!

Heading for Kingmoor shed, we immediately noticed the difference to previous visits, with stored engines scattered everywhere and of all shapes, sizes and quality. This was to be a common feature wherever we went over the next week.

In retrospect, we had taken a chance on the driving, as I was the only one to have passed a test! Peter and Les could not drive at all and David was still taking his lessons; he was to be my co-driver! But in blissful anticipation, we set off and, by and large, all went well, despite the steering which had a dangerous habit of wandering, the 6-volt lights hardly seeing anything at night, the wipers stopping whenever I put my foot on the accelerator and the engine barely able to handle the weight of four youths and their luggage! But in the whole week we had only two minor incidents – a flat tyre and a flat battery; the latter because I left the lights on overnight. That is, apart from one silly episode at Dawsholm when, on preparing to leave the shed, I was blatantly showing off my driving skills in cavalier fashion and reversed into a set of buffer stops! The dent in the boot did nothing to improve the car's appearance, nor did it help the operation of the boot flap and retrieval of cases!

The first night we stayed at a house in Ayr and the following night in Ardrossan. How we found the lodgings, I cannot remember, but in Ardrossan the 'landlady' had recently lost her husband and she was very nervous at accepting the presence of four dodgy looking youths! Her friend persuaded her, also that 10pm was too early to expect us to come in; we were thus given strict instructions to be in by 11pm – prompt – and we were not to be drunk! We spent the evening at the very primitive Ardrossan bowling alley!

Hurlford shed had been a scene of some dereliction and so were Ardrossan and Greenock; both shadows of their former selves, with the latter having just one engine – 42216 – in steam. And Kilmarnock Works was an indispensable visit – 80111 being the only engine in sight! It was pleasing to see 54463 still

around, at Carstairs, but, sadly, very much in store; and the line of stored locos at Bathgate, including 60042 *Singapore*, was a depressing sight. Corkerhill was bare by comparison to former visits, and Polmadie was a transformation – out of 66 (only) engines on shed, only 28 were steam, of which 3 were ragged and many others looked very cold indeed.

Having planned more sheds in the Glasgow area for Day 4, we checked into a cheap hotel in the city for the night and I parked outside. We found a local bar in which to spend the evening, noticed the complete lack of females in it and had just got settled when the landlord called 'Time' – it was only 10 o'clock! Walking back to the hotel, I noticed I was parked in a restricted zone, and so got up at the crack of dawn to move the car. It was pouring with rain and the nearest parking I could find was nearly a mile away! Getting soaked before breakfast was not my idea of fun and neither was being despatched, when ready to leave, to fetch the car, coming back to pick up the others. I was soaked twice! Fortunately, the rain stopped early during the morning (it is not easy writing down numbers in soggy notebooks) and the day improved – that is, until that Dawsholm incident! We arrived outside St Rollox Works, 10 minutes ahead of our due time, but the Works' party leader was waiting for us and shouted to us to hurry up, before I had the time to switch off the engine! We were hustled, a little breathless, inside the building. It was moderately interesting in there, but absolutely no steam. It was a pleasure to reach the shed and see 45374 of Aston shed and obviously just ex-Works, and 45742 *Connaught*, still very much in work. *Connaught* lasted another nine months only.

We had planned to stay at our old haunt in Perth, but it had changed hands; however, the present incumbent directed us around the corner, to a bank manager's house! The manager was away, but his wife agreed to let us stay – again, after some nervous eyeing us up and down!

On Day 5, we contented ourselves with the morning at Hilton Junction, just south of Perth, where the routes for Glasgow and Edinburgh split (*see colour Plate 4*); and the afternoon visiting Aberdeen, where we stayed overnight. It was a more relaxing day and we all needed the rest, as well as enjoying seeing the workings at the Junction. On the approaches to Aberdeen, the steering was pushed close to its limits as, on a long steep hill downwards, we were being menaced from behind by a very large lorry. He obviously wanted to go faster than I, so put pressure on me to speed up. The Ford was quickly topping 60mph (a lot for that car) and, with the steering having great fun, we wildly zigzagged down the hill. The lorry driver must have thought I was deliberately trying to prevent him overtaking me – if only he knew!! When we reached Aberdeen, I was wringing with sweat and near mental and physical exhaustion, with my arms aching from the exertions!

Working our way south on Day 6, we called in at Montrose and although only three engines were there – 64597, 64558 and 64577 – they were all in steam and it was a delightful little place.

Our stay that night was in Edinburgh (not in the station Waiting Room this time!) and we did the tourist bit to the Castle in the evening, just missing the end of a performance of the Tattoo. The weather, by this time, had become the complete opposite to the west side of the country, where we had started, and was now brilliant sunshine and marvellous sunsets.

Day 7 was our last in Scotland and it was with much sadness again, and regret, that we headed south, calling in at Hawick, Tweedmouth, Alnmouth and North Blyth, before spending the night at Whitley Bay. Our final day of this holiday started by us revisiting one of my favourite sheds, Heaton, but, again, the transformation was dramatic – 29 on shed, 21 steam, but only 60940 and 60946 not in store; it was heartbreaking to see A4 60002 *Sir Murrough Wilson* in the storeline. Tyne Dock, Sunderland and Consett were some improvement (the latter without the snow this time) and Darlington was home to a few steam engines just ex-Works. David was cock-a-hoop at seeing 60530 *Sayajirao* on shed in the evening sunshine and to have the opportunity of photographing it.

After this mammoth trek – and bearing in mind the driving problems – one would have thought we would want to rest; but no. Having just had two days' break, we set off for South Wales, to spend six days touring the valleys! The beauty of the freedom given us by the car was proved as we visited all manner of little places, that would otherwise have been impossible. New ground was broken at Dowlais Central (with just 5618 present), Ferndale (5613), Aberdare and Llantrisant (closed a month after our visit). We nearly did not reach Wales at all, however, as on the journey down we found ourselves in the middle of an Army convoy. Travelling at some speed down country roads, I had the window wide open to enjoy the summer sun; unfortunately, a wasp decided to hitch a ride. Buzzing round my head, I tried avoiding action and caught the steering wheel. We swung off the road, up a grass bank and back down again in a matter of seconds, resuming our place in the convoy! How the car stayed upright, or I did not hit anything, I shall never know – the wasp flew out in fright!

An obvious lodging place was the guest house in Barry and it was like being back home, we were made to feel so welcome. The engines on the Docks had moved around a little but, scattered over all sorts of places, in sidings, etc, nearer the main running lines, were all manner of 'new' engines. As well as more GW locos, there were some Southern and four Midland – 48431, 53809, 53808 and 45690 *Leander*, stripped of front number and nameplates. Southern was also present at Swansea East Dock (in the guise of 33010, 31917 and 33014) on 2 September; at Severn Tunnel Junction, on 4 September (31913 and 30107); and at Cashmore's Scrap Yard in Newport (31623). At this stage, the latter yard was vying with Woodham's for GW engines, but over the next few years would cut MR and SR locos as well as 'Standards'.

On Barry shed the allocation had dwindled and D6935, on 2 September, was a precursor of things to come. This holiday was also a precursor of changes for me. On 3 and 5 September we took days off for non-railway pursuits and though I did not know it at the time, this would be the last railway-only holiday I would take.

The reason for this was Gill. Having now worked with her for nearly a year, we had become very close and she announced that she would give up her current boyfriend, to go with me. It was decided he be told on Sunday, 4 October, and we would begin together the following day. The 4th coincided with a special charter train, to run through Grantham and to be hauled by a 'Semi'. My mind was not fully on this as Peter and I travelled to Grantham station and I was, therefore, not too concerned that the engine was in fact 70020 *Mercury*. I took little notice of the diesels that either hung around the station area or flashed past (steam had been eliminated by this date) and thought only of the Monday morning. Would she tell him? It seemed an eternity to her arrival at the office and she kept me in suspense for some time – but she had told him. One pre-condition of the courtship, however, was that she took an interest in trains (!) and she therefore joined me the following Sunday on a trip to revisit Didcot, Swindon, Bristol and Gloucester. What she thought of it, I am not sure, but she seemed happy enough.

1964 closed with my nine-year tally now 15,584 (12,285 steam).

54. *Top* The big snows of early 1963 surround 69461 as she stands forlorn on Stratford shed on 3 February. Her 'chimney' and valve on the dome betray the fact that she has been used as a stationary boiler; she was withdrawn from normal service in June 1954 and her years of non-movement (and obvious lack of attention) are evidenced by 'NER' beginning to show through on her tank!

55. *Bottom* Caught in the act! Captured by the camera, I lead our small raiding party into the yard of North Blyth shed on Sunday, 17 February 1963. The appalling and bitter weather conditions can be seen from the snow, sky and abundance of steam around 62022. LES WADE

56 & 57. Casualties of Darlington Works on Saturday, 16 February 1963.

Top Both these two V2s had been withdrawn only in December 1962, but 60807 and 60879 have both been very quickly reduced to scrap, as can be judged from the accumulation of snow against the former. LES WADE

Bottom A young member of our group stands transfixed, as the steam crane winches part of 64758 into the air. She had been withdrawn in November 1962 and 64835 one month later. Darlington certainly wasted no time in cutting! LES WADE

58. *Above* Incredibly, although the shed was surrounded by large amounts of snow, the inside of Tyne Dock's roofless roundhouse seems clear of it! Q6s 63411 and 63393 make a pleasing sight, in drab surroundings, as they await their next duties, Sunday, 17 February 1963.

59. *Top right* The infamous view at Goole on Sunday, 30 March 1963. D6733 still smoulders, having been set on fire the day before by so-called 'steam enthusiasts'. We got no closer to the shed than this shot, which shows 90186, D2598, 90704 and 43125 in company with the Type 3. LES WADE

60. *Bottom right* Seventy-two years old and still going strong, 11368 (still carrying her old Midland number, despite being allocated 51368 by BR) shunts 52515 and 47402, in Horwich Works, 21 April 1963. LES WADE

61. *Top* Another shed-bashing trip and a very early morning start at Banbury, where 5990 *Dorford Hall* makes her leisurely way past the shed yard, 28 April 1963.

62. *Bottom* Compared to *Dorford Hall*, 6983 *Otterington Hall* a 'Modified Hall' – a Hawksworth development of Collett's original. She prepares to leave the confines of Didcot shed on April 1963.

63. *Top* The WR 5700 Class was a delightful design, eminently functional, but also aesthetically very pleasing. A total of 829 were built over a twenty-year period and they lasted through to the end of steam on the Western Region. 3751 looks in good shape on Didcot shed, 28 April 1963.

64. *Bottom* As well as the FA Cup, Rugby League's Cup Finals also produced Specials, many of which used the Central route. A Wakefield-Marylebone Excursion is seen passing Leicester South Goods behind 45658 *Keyes* of Holbeck shed, 11 May 1963. HORACE GAMBLE

65. *Above* After an extensive fire had all but destroyed Preston shed, it ceased to be an active depot and became, for a while, a repository for stored engines. During this period, unrebuilt 'Patriots' graced the shed confines and 45543 *Home Guard* is seen, ragged up in the late afternoon sun of 9 June 1963.

66. *Top right* I was delighted to see 1151 on Swansea East Dock shed on 30 June 1963, as I found the South Wales saddle-tanks fascinating. I was even more pleased that she stood out in the open, enabling me to photograph her. I was sad to learn that she was withdrawn six weeks later.

67. *Bottom right* The next day, 1 July, saw me visiting Ebbw Junction shed in Newport, where 92222 lets off some steam, before moving off to pick up her next trainload.

68. *Top* Stoke shed was a mixture of roundhouse and straight buildings, with some distance between them. 42542 stands in the former on 14 July 1963.

69. *Bottom* Some of the power of 73026 can be judged from this view, as she 'hides' round the side of Shrewsbury shed, 14 July 1963.

70. *Top* Never with a large allocation or presence, the Southern shed at Reading did, however, give a nice contrast to the GW engines close by. On Sunday, 20 October 1963, 31857 stands in the yard, with the GW main line in the background.

71. *Bottom* In steam days a visit to Swindon Works always provided the spectacle of spotless engines, just ex-Works. 7803 *Barcote Manor* is an immaculate case in point, glistening on the afternoon of 20 October 1963.

72. *Top* Another intriguing view from Swindon Works, this time showing 8102 apparently converted into an 0-4-0T, standing outside the A-Shop, 10 May 1964.

73. *Bottom* 04/8 63726 is not to move again, as she is already withdrawn, standing in Retford GC yard on 14 June 1964. By the state of her buffer and running plate, she has seen some hard work!

74. *Top* It was always interesting to visit Wath, to see the Woodhead electrics and 14 June 1964 was no exception. 26022 stands in line with a number of her sisters, all looking in good shape.

75. *Bottom* In 1964, although nominally an ER depot, Canklow housed a wide variety of engines, including 'Jubilee' 45721 *Impregnable*, on 14 June.

76. *Above* Staveley GC was a cold and draughty shed to visit, even in summer. 63701, although tabbed 'Not to be moved', was only temporarily becalmed, as she and 63725 (*right*) both survived another twelve months, 14 June 1964.

77. *Top right* A view of Leicester (15C) shed in the transition period, when both steam and diesel were at work. 92102 and 92104 stand in company with D5227 and D5405 – the latter subsequently disappeared to work out its life in Scotland.

78. *Bottom right* There seems to be some consternation about the state of 4613, seen at the rear of Worcester shed, during our 'railtour' visit of 12 July 1964.

79. *Above* 31400 looks as though she had stopped very abruptly, shooting her innards out of the smokebox door! Perhaps of more interest is B1 61313; the reason for her presence on 19 July 1964 I never did discover.

80. *Top right* The troupe of trainspotters can be seen anxious to get to 34093 *Saunton*, having already put 33004 into their books. Guildford, 19 July 1964.

81. *Bottom right* Another Scottish holiday and 'Crabs' were everywhere on Ayr shed during our visit of 23 August 1964. 42861, however, appears to be trying to be a little exclusive!

82. *Top* Just some of the multitude of engines scattered around Barry Docks can be seen in this view of 48354 delivering a couple more, 2 September 1964.

83. *Bottom* A sad photo. 5668 is the last steam engine to be present on Barry shed, ousted by Type 3 diesels seen alongside. She awaits removal, on 6 September 1964.

84. *Top* A bright but hazy sunshine illuminates Grantham station, as 70020 *Mercury* enters on a Home Counties Railway Society tour (in place of the advertised engine), 4 October 1964.

85. *Bottom* Steam engines were not meant to withstand the heat of an oil train fire, but that is precisely what overtook 48734, seen dumped at the back of Didcot shed, 11 October 1964. Not surprisingly, she never worked again!

CHAPTER FOUR

With the spreading elimination of steam, it was becoming increasingly difficult to find new or different places to go. Although my camera was now light years ahead of what I had started with, I had no interest or enthusiasm in capturing diesels or electrics on film. Not only had they replaced steam, but it seemed they would be around, unchanged, for many years to come; and, anyway, they were nowhere near as aesthetically satisfying. In retrospect how wrong I was, both on this assumption and in adopting the selective posture, photographing only steam. I would have been better advised to snap anything that moved; considering how permanent steam had once seemed, I was painfully slow to realise the facts of life. Thankfully, I have since learned!

Unlike other years, in 1965 I did not venture forth until March when, on the 7th, Gill and I travelled to Norwich – by way of New England. I had, by now, graduated to a Morris 1000 which, in comparison to the Ford, was sheer luxury and was distinctly more comfortable to drive long distances (and with straight steering!).

There were a handful of bedraggled-looking steam engines at New England – all in store, of course – but none at Norwich; or, at least, none that we saw, as we were summarily chased from the shed! On the way back, we called in at King's Scrap Yard in Hall Road, Norwich. Unlike his BR counterpart, the foreman at King's was most accommodating and helpful and I was able to find 33033, 30546, 33006, 33003, 33030, 31827 and 31400. The latter two were interesting, as they had been together on Redhill shed during our visit of 19 July 1964.

On 28 March TRS made a trip to Manchester, visiting Stockport, Heaton Mersey, Longsight, Trafford Park, Patricroft, Agecroft, Newton Heath and Gorton. It was now virtually impossible to tell which engines were still normally in service and which were in store. There was no attempt at emptying the bunkers/tenders of coal; engines were seemingly just left dumped, possibly to work again, possibly not. Two exceptions to this were 45522 *Prestatyn* and 44425 at Buxton; minus chimneys, it was fairly certain they had worked their last! (*see Plate 89*)

One good thing from these two trips was that Gill seemed to bring good weather with her and this continued throughout most of the year on our various outings, although the non-railway ones were on the increase. The general enthusiasm within TRS was declining, with the decrease in viable locations and the above trip to Manchester proved to be my last at the helm; after that, David took over and I joined for only a couple of trips.

It was now back to individual initiative, which I next took on 20 June by taking Gill for a weekend to my haunt at Barry. The shed was now totally diesel – D6829, D6971, D6949, D6929, D6974, D6838 and D6835 were present on that day – and there were now more than ever on the Docks and surroundings: a total of 116!

It was becoming a scramble to see steam working wherever possible; to find areas where there were enough locations close by each other to make the trip worthwhile; to see the last this or that; to maintain interest. Increasingly, scrap yards were included in the itinerary, as on 25 July, when Cashmore's at Great Bridge was visited, between viewing Nuneaton and Bescot sheds. We were chased out of both of the latter, also Oxley which was next, but the day improved at Stourbridge and Tyseley. Asked many years later what her overriding impressions were of those days, Gill's immediate reaction was 'Being chased out of sheds!' I had not realised it had been that often!

As some consideration for her, we planned a 'normal' holiday for 1965 and joined my parents in their trip to the Isle of Wight. But, lo and behold, there was still steam *and* it was virgin territory for me! The weather was super (most of the time) and ideal for trainspotting – Mum and Dad hardly saw us, as I dragged Gill round the Island's network. We did spend one or two days on the beach out of a fortnight but, with the weather being so good, the sand was far too hot! On 19 August I decided we would make the trip from Yarmouth, by ferry to Lymington, travel to Brockenhurst and Bournemouth and back. There was some initial resistance, but having insisted, we had a good day – except that it poured with rain all day; some form of Divine retribution, no doubt! Our Holiday Special trains (both out and back) took an interesting route – from Leicester, via Market Harborough, Northampton, Bletchley, Oxford, Reading, Basingstoke, Eastleigh, to Portsmouth; and outwards we were hauled by D1574 to Oxford, and then 6991 *Acton Burnell Hall*; with the return being D6548 to Oxford, and then D5860 back to Leicester.

Twenty years on and enthusiasts would queue up for such a trip!

Back home in Leicester, attention focused on the Great Central, which was in its death throes. The main line now only ran from Marylebone to Nottingham and 'Britannias' had been drafted in, in an attempt to improve the running of the service. In September, 70046 *Anzac*, 70052 *Firth of Tay* and 70054 *Dornoch Firth* were new appearances and they caused a great deal of interest among the cognoscenti. Apart from this, with no organised trips I was forced onto outings such as a day trip to Birmingham on 23 October, which at least did produce steam, at both New Street and Snow Hill. I also had to exist on odd items of interest, like the sight of E6009 being towed through Leicester, behind D7516. The year for me as a trainspotter was quietly dying and, statistically this is shown with me copping a mere 75 steam.

With outside interests now increasingly encroaching on my time, it was March before we attempted any 1966 trips, with us going north on the 6th, to Kirkby-in-Ashfield, Langwith Junction, Staveley, Chesterfield, Westhouses and Derby. We had purposely ended up there, as 60019 *Bittern* was due to haul a William's Deacons Bank Railway Club Special through the town. It was a mad dash throughout the day, to be in place, just south of Derby station at the appointed hour, but we made it and the sun came out to grace our endeavours. (*see colour Plate 7*) Compared to a similar charter in the 1980s, there were few cameras about – most people preferring to actually travel on the train – and what cameraman there were, were most concerned that they did not intrude on others' photographs. Would that it were so today!

Increasingly, now, my 'extra-mural studies' were gaining preference, with the football team I ran taking up more of my time; there was also the Drama Group; and Gill wanted to do other things, not unnaturally, like going to see Bob Dylan in concert, at the DeMontfort Hall in Leicester on 15 May. We were interviewed and filmed outside the theatre by some of his entourage. We were asked whether we would boo him, as some others had done, for his transition from acoustic to electric music. 'No way,' we quickly said; as the second half of his show deteriorated into noisy cacophony, we were to eat our words!

Our 1966 rail trips were severely limited – to Barry again, for a weekend at the end of April; and little more than flying visits to the Birdcage, the Central or Melton Mowbray (near to where Gill lived), until our holiday in August. Again with Mum and Dad, we went to Colwyn Bay, which did at least have a railway and on the coast – not too unlike Dawlish. Although the majority of services were diesel hauled, there was still quite a healthy amount of steam and not only was it good to see, it helped reawaken the slumbering interest. So much so, that on 16 August we set off to travel on the Festiniog Railway. Having caught the train to Llandudno Junction and then to Blaenau Festiniog, we hopped on a bus to Tan-y-Bwlch, which was then the northern terminus of the railway – and without any platforms! Not a bit like the scene of

prosperity, twenty years later! From Porthmadog, we caught a bus to Caernarvon, from where we trained to Bangor and caught our connection back to Colwyn. A day graced by yet more bright sunshine, it was most satisfying all round; the only time I would travel from Caernarvon to Bangor by rail; and most of it, even on BR, was behind steam.

A fortnight after this, on 3 September, normal steam finished in Leicester, with the closure of the Great Central to Marylebone. 35030 *Elder Dempster Lines* ran a special, to mark the occasion, but worked the return leg too late, through Leicester Central, for satisfactory photography; 45292 worked in on the last service from London; and that was it. Rumoured and talked of for so long, the end had come with abrupt suddenness, leaving a numbness that would last a long time.

Steam returned to the Midland a week later, in the shape of 4472 *Flying Scotsman*, now preserved (*see colour Plate 8*), on a special, but it was not the same. The next visit of steam to the city, though, was much better and the highlight of the year.

On 3 December Gill and I joined an excursion to Carlisle and back, setting out in the darkness of 7am, behind 45562 *Alberta*. It had been a toss-up as to whether Roger – who had joined us at the Bank in Syston and who was a keen railway enthusiast – or I would go, as one of us was required to work that Saturday morning. Thankfully, I won!

Travelling through Sheffield, we headed further north to Mirfield, where *Alberta* came off and sister engine 45593 *Kolhapur* took over. We then took the Hebden Bridge line to Blackburn, Lostock Hall and Preston, where the 'Jubilee' looked a fine sight, in the bright winter's sunshine, heading out of the town under the huge signal gantry that then stood proudly, just north of the station. From here, *Kolhapur* stormed her way to Carlisle, over Shap and then proceeded to take us right into the Kingmoor yard. Thankfully, steam was still in abundance, with few diesels, and it was almost back to the good old days. The route back was via Leeds and Derby, where David and Barbara (his girlfriend) joined us on the train (unofficially), for the final run to Leicester. The day was magic, with one small flaw. I had put my head out of the window sometime before Preston and had received a cinder in the eye for my pains (shades of Les!). It would not go away and irritated all day. When we got back to Leicester, my next trip was straight into the Out-Patients department of the Royal Infirmary!

This trip and Christmas were most enjoyable and Gill and I planned for 1967's holiday. Early in January we decided (with a little encouragement from me) on Dawlish and booked for a fortnight. Within days I had broken off our relationship for reasons I have never been able to explain fully. Gill was upset, to say the least, and could not understand my demented reasoning. Truth to tell, neither could I, but I wrote cancelling her room, but keeping mine; deep down I had a feeling that we would get back together in time for the holiday – but it was not to be. I had no idea what sort of holiday I would have! To keep my mind occupied, I made more regular trips to Kettering where now, almost exclusively, the scrap yard was dealing with MR freight engines. On 4 March I joined a Leicester City football special to Wolverhampton and sat on the station all the afternoon – the returning fans thought it very strange that I did not know the score – and I began spotting trips again. Roger had, by now, organised a small group and I joined them for the first time, on 7 May, on a trip to London.

I had not visited Hitchin or Hornsey sheds before and, therefore, was glad to be going there and only sorry that it was after steam days. The latter proved very interesting with 30 engines present; as, too, did Finsbury Park, which followed. The Deltics looked big and powerful at the head of trains; viewed from ground level, on shed, they were even bigger and D9015 *Tulyar* really did make D5908 look a 'Baby' Deltic! Stratford was its usual fascinating self, albeit, all diesel, but there was some steam, in the form of preserved engines: 1008, 70000 *Britannia*, 30245, 33001, 42500, 30777 *Sir Lamiel*, 63460, 30587, 30925 *Cheltenham*, 63601, 120, 30850 *Lord Nelson*, and 49395. It is interesting to see the various points of the compass to which these have since travelled. Hither Green, Old Oak and Willesden were exclusively electric, diesel, and both (!), but Nine Elms had only one diesel present – D3273 – out of 27 locos present on shed. At this time, the Southern was the only region flying the steam flag to any degree and the sight of this predominance of the old warhorses was truly heart-warming. There was one diesel of note on this trip – 10001; then still on Willeseden shed, withdrawal had been over a year beforehand. She eventually met her end, in February 1968, at Cox & Dank's Scrap Yard in North Acton.

The next trip was on 1 July and, although it was not exactly like the old times, at least I was travelling more than in the recent past.

This time we turned the compass north and hit the North-East which, like the Southern and, indeed, the North-West, was still healthily endowed with working steam; except for Blyth, which had much of its allocation in store. Elsewhere, although grimy and often needing attention, steam battled on, but the likes of 90254 did not help themselves by jumping the tracks in West Hartlepool's shed yard and leaning at a crazy angle! Whilst walking round the yard, I was overjoyed to see D173 pass on a passenger turn – it was my last 'Peak', and the feeling of elation was definitely similar to that on Bank Hall, with *Glorious*. Later that day, York was mostly diesel, but Holbeck and Wakefield were still predominantly steam, albeit some of it out of action; and, indeed, Wakefield seemed to have become something of a dumping ground.

The day after this, I joined David, Barbara and Chirp, for a dash south, to locations at Beaulieu Road, Lyndhurst and Basingstoke, to witness the very last days of steam on the Southern; much had changed in the two months since the visit to Nine Elms! 34095 *Brentor*, 35008 *Orient Line* and 35028 *Clan Line*, were all in good health as they handled their expresses for the last time, but already they were devoid of front

numbers and nameplates – a complete contrast to earlier times, when engines were stored still bearing all. During the day, I invited Chirp to join me in Dawlish – but he thought Gill and I would get back together and declined. We did not, though, and on 12 August I caught the train at Leicester, bound for the Devon coast.

A girl I knew from the Bank was catching the same train and I joined her and her two companions for the journey. This was a mistake!

For myself, I was intent on recording as many numbers as possible on the way, as well as being sociable, but we were joined (forcibly) by a trio of pseudo-Hell's Angels, who insisted the blind be pulled down; they did not take kindly to my alternative suggestions! Although they were only interested in the girls, they (the girls) were not particularly interested in these interlopers and tensions mounted as the journey progressed. I was relieved to arrive at Dawlish and detrain!

Staying at the same seafront hotel as some years earlier, I was made most welcome although it had changed hands. I had anticipated a lonely holiday, without Gill or anyone else to accompany me, but I made friends in the hotel with a couple of holidaying spotters from Hull and also made the acquaintance of eleven different girls in the fortnight! I left one in tears on Dawlish station on my return, and another in the same state at Birmingham New Street. This girl I befriended in the hour between my trains and, catching a train to Weston-Super-Mare, she almost changed trains and came home with me! Thus, with the seafront railway; sun, sea and sand; and a trip to the emergent Dart Valley Railway, I had a super holiday and the better for being all totally unexpected.

Still high from this, two days later, I drove Roger up to Westhouses and Langwith Junction – just to see what was there; and then, on 3 September, Peter joined me for a trip to Stoke and Crewe. Unfortunately, the weather changed for the worse for this trip and all day we were treated to a continual, soaking drizzle.

The two of us returned to Crewe again on 7 October, on the way to the North-west for the weekend. It was now obvious that steam would be wiped out completely within months and I determined to see and photograph as much as possible. There was, indeed, much to see and, happily, much was still hard at work albeit on freight rather than passenger duties. We travelled as far as Blackpool, where 70021 *Morning Star* was resplendent on shed on the Sunday morning; and then made our way back via Rose Grove and Bolton. The presence on these two sheds was surprisingly high – 41 and 43 respectively and much of it still in steam. Sutton Oak, Speke and Edge Hill were much the same and it was almost like being in a time warp, compared to the rest of the country; and Birkenhead was incredible, with 65 engines in and around the shed area – and no bricks!

A month later, I was back at Crewe yet again and those sheds in the North-West, but what transformations.

Birkenhead looked nude – only 12 engines present; whilst Northwich had swollen to 31 and Springs Branch (Wigan) from 62 to 80. It was almost as if we were playing railway musical chairs! Considering how close the time was then to the end of steam and admitting that some of the statistics are diesels, the tally for locos seen that day was:–

Crewe South	–	77
Crewe Diesel	–	10
Northwich	–	31
Birkenhead	–	12
Edge Hill	–	52
Speke	–	81
Sutton Oak	–	23
Springs Branch	–	80
Bolton	–	37
Newton Heath	–	69
Patricroft	–	59
Trafford Park	–	36
Heaton Mersey	–	20
Stockport	–	34
Buxton	–	25

Having now done the area three times in as many months and with nowhere else to go – or, certainly, nowhere of any great interest to me – I sat back for the winter. Early spring saw me out again and back to Barry, where there were still more additions – I logged 214 engines on 17 March.

By this time, I had again changed my car to an Austin 1100 and had a new girlfriend. Anna-Maria was of Italian extraction and worked with David. It was natural, therefore, that we went out as a foursome and logical that she should come along on a trip to Carnforth, Lostock Hall and Blackpool, on 15 April 1968. Carnforth housed another chimney-less engine – 45209 – but much was still in steam; and Lostock Hall was temporary home to D403, then still a rare class to us. Anna-Maria took David's and my comments and excitement in her stride and she was a good companion; except for her pouring her coffee over me at Blackpool (by accident)!?!

Around this time, steam re-appeared in Leicester, with the shed roundhouse being home to 4771 *Green Arrow*, 44027, 63601 and 49395; (the last two had followed me from Stratford). There were plans to house them in a new Museum of Technology in the city, but these came to naught.

And so the year dragged on and the fateful final day of steam on BR arrived. Peter and I had cleared our weekend in order to travel and stay in the North-West, to be on hand at the death. We did many of the usual sheds and there still seemed to be a fair amount of breath left in the monsters, but none more so than at Lostock Hall, where preparations were being made with the last run engines.

On 'Black Sunday' – 4 August (the day after my twenty-fifth birthday) – the early morning scene, in the bright sunshine, was of a level of activity that probably had not been witnessed in years. There were railmen, officials and spotters everywhere and especially around the showpiece, 70013 *Oliver Cromwell*. It is doubtful whether she had looked better for many days in her whole career. A small handful of Black Fives were also being made ready, but they were almost also-rans alongside the star!

Eventually they left the depot, took up their final duties, kept thousands of cameras happy and, at the end of the day, finally died, along with all other 'real' steam. The steam age, once so permanent and relatively unloved, was ended.

It was a dreadful feeling of bewilderment and estrangement; rather like losing an arm. What could we do with ourselves without the regular 'injection' of spotting steam? I joined Roger and his group on 16 November on a trip to the then infant Keighley & Worth Valley Railway and I dutifully logged the numbers there and at Healey Mills, Wath, Darnall, Staveley and Westhouses – but it was not the same and it was not just the dull weather that created the feeling of disappointment and despair.

But, on the personal front, things had moved.

I had begun free-lance writing in the music field, with a regular column in *Syston Times* (and its syndicates); I had started the Leicestershire Blues Appreciation Society to further my interest in and knowledge of blues music; I had appeared on Radio Leicester; and on 22 December I had met Judith. Over Christmas I spoke to her by phone, and on New Year's Eve she joined me for a blues concert that I had organised. Eighteen months later she was my wife!

Truly, as one door closed . . . !

86. *Top* Although retaining its front number, B1 61272 had been withdrawn from capital stock for two months at the date of this photograph and had become Departmental Locomotive No 25, to be a stationary boiler at New England shed. Steaming gaily there on 7 March 1965, she was finally withdrawn in November of that year.

87. *Bottom* Neither loco nor railmen appear to be working too hard, as a very clean 48344 slowly passes Trafford Park shed and football ground, 28 March 1965.

88. *Top* 'Honour your partners!' Lamps and water cranes seem to be preparing to dance in a bare Trafford Park yard, 28 March 1965.

89. *Bottom* Patriot 45522 *Prestatyn* and 44425 'deep in conversation' over who has 'lifted' their chimneys? Buxton, 28 March 1965.

90 & 91. Two views of the Great Central in the closing years.

Top In an attempt to save costs and the truncated services, English Electric Type 3s were drafted in and D67XX heads north, through the afternoon sunshine, past Belgrave & Birstall box, on 5 June 1965.

Bottom Black Five 45299 passes Leicester North Goods with a morning Nottingham Victoria-Marylebone semi-fast, on 7 August 1965. Where the train is, became a footpath in the 1980s, and the lines on the extreme right ended up in Vic Berry's scrapyard empire. HORACE GAMBLE

Two views from the holiday in the Isle of Wight in 1965.

92. *Top* On a day trip to Bournemouth, some time was spent at Brockenhurst on the return, whilst waiting for the branch train to Lymington. Unfortunately, the weather deteriorated as we waited and the rain fell heavily, shortly after this view taken of 80134 on a branch train, 19 August 1965.

93. *Bottom* Part of the charm of the Island was the diminutive Adams 02s, No 35 *Freshwater*, fitted for push-pull working, prepares to leave Ryde station with a train for Ventnor, 24 August 1965.

94. *Above* On a dull and cold 6 March 1966, D1749 heads a 'down' express out of Chesterfield, past a small collection of steam engines awaiting scrap, including 61361.

95. *Top right* Where else but Barry Docks?! In the mid-Sixties views like this became commonplace as thousands trekked to pay homage. 34070 *Manston* heads a row, with 9629 and 3612 behind and 5541 to the right, 20 April 1966.

96. *Bottom right* When steam had finished on the Midland main line, I did not feel inclined to photograph diesels, but the En-Tout-Cas Works at Thurmaston, to the north of Leicester, makes for an interesting backdrop to D7656 heading north, 10 September 1966.

97. *Above* Heading north, on a Leicester-Carlisle Special, I am not the only one photographing the superb signal gantry at the north end of Preston station. 'Jubilee' 45593 *Kolhapur* works hard, gathering speed on the outward trip, on 3 December 1966.

98. *Top right* Part of the joy of 35mm film was the greater flexibility for experimentation. 'Jinty' 47396 is glimpsed through the buffers of wagons, all waiting to be cut up, at Cohen's yard, Kettering, on 25 February 1967.

99. *Bottom right* 'Deltics' looked big and powerful at the head of their trains, but close to they were even mightier. Showing some of this size, D9019 *Royal Highland Fusilier* stands proudly on Finsbury Park shed, 7 May 1967.

100. *Left* In 1967 Stratford shed was home to several preserved steam locos. A row of them are viewed by Roger from the footplate of 70000 *Britannia*, on 7 May.

101. *Top right* Living in the Midlands, Southern electrics were rare beasts. I was therefore pleased to photograph prototype E6001, standing with sister E6031 on Hither Green depot, on 7 May 1967.

102. *Bottom* Despite widespread dieselisation, Nine Elms fought bravely for steam to the end. Sadly, 73022 will not work again, having just been withdrawn and lacking connecting rods. Neither will 80012 work again, but 35023 *Holland-Afrika Line* will live on a couple more months, 7 May 1967.

103. *Top* The sight of forlorn rows of abandoned steam engines became common, such as that containing 43071, 62062 and many others at North Blyth, 1 July 1967.

104. *Bottom* Shafts of sunlight make a pleasing sight inside Sunderland shed on 1 July 1967, as 65855 stands in the company of 65811 and 65894.

105. *Top* Fitting the twilight of steam on SR, the shadows stretch long at Basingstoke on 2 July 1967, catching 73018 with 80152.

106. *Bottom* Looking for all the world as if it has run through a wall leaving cab and tender behind, 45276 is surrounded by debris at Kettering, 30 July 1967.

107. Another slightly unusual view of an oft-photographed coastline. Double-headed Westerns pass between tunnels on the outskirts of Dawlish on an 'up' express, 15 August 1967.

108. Although not working, 4555 looks incredibly authentic, at
the head of a train in Buckfastleigh Station on the preserved
Dart Valley Railway, 22 August 1967.

109 & 110. Contrasts in shed scenes.
Top The sun shines brightly on a very healthy presence at Crewe South on 3 September 1967, with 92233, 48522 and 48725 standing at the head of their rows, near to the main line.

Bottom Nearly a year later and the sky cries at the approach of the end of steam! 73069 (*far left*) and 48773 stand in a downpour at the entrance to Bolton shed in the early summer of 1968.

111. *Top* The last weekend of steam. Peter photographs the graffiti on the smokebox door of 48390, whilst 73143 looks on, Patricroft, 2 August 1968.

112. *Bottom* The death of an engine. The crew of 45342 smile as they leave their charge, shunted into the siding of Carnforth shed for the last time, to be left for the fire to go out, to work no more. 3 August 1968.

113. The very last day and 70013 *Oliver Cromwell* literally
gleams in the very early morning of 4 August 1968, in company
with 45110 on Lostock Hall shed, awaiting their calls to haul the
last Specials.

CHAPTER FIVE

1969 saw me transferred back into the centre of Leicester by the Bank; engaged to Judith; increasing my writing outlets, for music; and developing the Blues Society. But such was the power of the railway drug, that wherever and whenever I was around the country, I was looking out for and writing down numbers, in what was to some extent a conditioned reflex. Thus it was, on an out-and-back visit to March, on 7 April and on the outward and return journeys of Judith's and my brief seven-day holiday in the Isle of Wight early in May (when I also dragged her up the hill out of Ventnor in the pouring rain to see the now-closed vandalised station buildings, she is still incredulous at the thought of this grown man almost in tears, over a broken-down railway station in the wet!); also on our weekend attending the 2nd National Blues Convention, in London.

But the pattern of interest *was* changing and the influence of steam was still overpowering. I had no inclination to continue pure spotting, to rush about all over the county, to clear off diesels, as I had once wanted to with steam. Instead, I turned my gaze towards the preservation movement. The obvious place was Loughborough and I watched with great interest the emerging of Main Line Steam Trust.

Judith had railway blood in her, as her Grandfather had worked in one of Leicester's signalboxes but, prior to meeting me, she had no great personal interest. She developed something of an interest, however, following our meeting, but she was most definitely a 'steam buff'. To her, then and now, diesels were not in the same league, devoid of life, and were to be regarded in much the same way as a car – a functional machine to transport people from one place to another. Thus, she was perfectly happy to visit preservation centres, to see 'working' steam; and then she had a chance to see still more steam at work, on honeymoon!

Travelling to Portugal, to spend a fortnight of post-wedding bliss with her Aunt and Uncle at their villa in the north in May 1970, I was intrigued to discover that steam was still in everyday use. I could not, in all honesty, expect Uncle and Aunt to chauffeur me around the country trainspotting, and so had to content myself with hoping to see something on the lines we kept crossing as we went out on our day trips. They were conscious of my interest and would have stopped had we seen anything but, in the first week, I

was fated to see virtually nothing; but things did improve in the second week, along with the weather, which did a complete U-turn, to become hot sunshine and clear blue skies. This rocketed the temperatures (which I found to my cost, as I rushed out to sunbathe – only to come out in a heat rash!) and we discovered just how hot it was on a trip to Santo Tirso.

Having finished our shopping, it was agreed that we would walk down to the station, which was about half-a-mile out of town. The walk there was not too bad, especially as there was a monastery and river to see on the way, but then we found that the next train was not due for nearly an hour. Short of just sitting on the platform, the only other alternative was to walk back (up the hill) to the town. This we did, feeling decidedly hotter every minute, then passed the time having a cup of coffee in the cool of a café. Nearer the appointed time, we began the hike back down the hill. The monastery and river now seemed somehow much less appealing. Very, very hot (and Judith and Aunt not a little bothered), we made the station, blissfully ignored the Portuguese signs forbidding us entry to the platform without a ticket (we could not read them could we?) and saw the train arrive, hauled by a quaint little tank, No E85. Betty, Judith's Aunt, was heard to mutter, 'Was it all worth it?' The sun was on the wrong side for photos from the platform, so we calmly walked across the tracks and snapped away, in a non-man's land between tracks – surprisingly, no one seemed to object; rather the opposite, as the driver and fireman abandoned the footplate to indulge in a frenzy of engine polishing! Whether this was purely for our benefit, I am not sure, but they certainly kept looking in our direction. After all this excitement, we dragged ourselves wearily back up the hill to the town, now feeling like wet rags and with my goodwill quotient having dropped several points!

After this, I had to pick outings with care and our next visit in the UK was to Tyseley on 13 September 1970. Lo and behold, what should be there, but dear old friends, 30777 *Sir Lamiel*, 30925 *Cheltenham*, 120 and 1008, plus 45428, 1501 and the stalwarts of the place, 7029 *Clun Castle* and 45593 *Kolhapur*. To see these two at work, resplendent in their burnished condition, was literally a feast for sore eyes!

Back in Leicester, *Green Arrow* was still housed in the old roundhouse, and long-preserved 118 and 158A had been moved into an old fire station on the southern outskirts of the city. A stranger place for a railway museum would be hard to find; it had absolutely no railway links whatever. On the real railway, the scene was dominated by 'Peaks' and Sulzer Type 2s (later Class 25). The earlier proliferation of Birmingham RC&W Co Type 2s (later Class 26 and 27) had now disappeared, with the locos having been dispersed to Scotland. Interestingly, some of them came back to Leicester in 1987 – to be scrapped by Vic Berry!

Although now very much a back seat occupation, the number habit was still there and on 31 March 1971 I was scribbbling away on a journey from Rayleigh to Leicester, via Liverpool Street and St Pancras, after a friend had given me a lift part-way back, on a journey home. The predominance on the trip to Liverpool Street, was clearly Brush Type 4s (Class 47) and 2/3s (Class 31). And the habit was still strong on a fortnight's canal holiday taken with Peter and his wife, Pam. Starting out from near Llangollen on 31 July, we had headed towards Macclesfield and, from the Ordnance Survey Map, there were various places where we came close to a railway. It was amazing how many mealtime stops seemed to coincide with us being at those places!

1972 was a poor year, with very few trips, but I did persuade Judith to take a run out on 29 May to sit by the lineside at Essendine. It was a dull, damp day and she was plainly bored, while I indulged in unashamed nostalgia, visualising A4s, A3s etc, sprinting up and down the bank. Having spent a couple of hours, during which time we had seen precisely 8 trains – 1863, 9015 *Tulyar*, 1507, 271, 9008 *The Green Howards*, 9011 *The Royal Northumberland Fusiliers*, 1506 and 341 and no photographs – we called it a day. Also, for the last half-an-hour there had been a strange man lurking near the car, hiding behind a workman's hut. I do not know what his intentions were, but he did not look at all savoury!

Our trip to Bridgnorth in October, though, was a much happier affair. Although not working, the stock was bathed in sunlight and this, plus time looking round the town, and a most enjoyable lunch, kept Judith happy. It was important to retain some domestic harmony!

1973 was BR's TOPS renumbering plans. If there had been a slow strangulation of my faltering interest in number-taking, this was the death blow. I had no enthusiasm for transferring all my collected numbers into a new book and for learning a whole new system, so I gave up. I still idly wrote down any recognisable ones I saw, like 6520 and 6521 at Weymouth, on our way to and from Guernsey in May, but when I saw 87003 in September and could not even recognise the Class, let alone the number, that was just too much!

I consoled myself with trips to Bressingham and Didcot on 16 and 23 September respectively, but it still was not the same; and the sight of half-dismantled engines at Parkend in June (and again in June 1974), did little to fill me with hope. I effectively 'hung up my boots' and admitted defeat and, if proof were needed, two trips in 1975 provided it.

In April, as part of the Bank's Nottingham District

Ten-Pin Bowling team, I travelled a return journey from Grantham to Newcastle. I know it was a 'Deltic' that hauled us north, but which one, I have not a clue; and David Taylor, one of our number, was avidly collecting numbers, delighted at what he saw at Doncaster and York – but I collected not one number on the whole journey. I was more interested in playing pontoon!, winning £13 on the outward journey and losing it all on the return! Then, early in October, Judith and I travelled to the United States to spend three weeks with Duane Eddy (that name again) to continue research for the biography I was writing. We travelled by rail to and from London but, again, not one number was recorded.

To all intents and purposes, the hobby was dead; the interest gone for ever. But, somehow, even after all this, it would not let me be entirely, as was to be proved the following year.

After the return from America we planned for a family and our first-born was due in October 1976. That summer, with Judith very big with child, we went to the North Yorks Moors, ostensibly for a (gentle) walking holiday. On the way north, we called in at York, to see the town and visit the Railway Museum. Outside the station, we heard a steam whistle! Hurrying onto the platform, we were met by the sight of *Flying Scotsman*, light engine. Talking to a couple of enthusiasts, we learned of a special, due in shortly, to be doubled-headed by *Hardwicke* and 92220 *Evening Star*! Immediately, all the old enthusiasm and excitement returned and Judith was caught up in a whirlwind as I rushed around the platforms, camera at the ready.

During the next fourteen days, we travelled extensively around the North Yorks Moors Railway (even dragging Judith and her stomach down what memory recalls as a near 1-in-2 hill at Levisham as a train approached!) and then called in at the Keighley & Worth Valley on the way home. What had been proposed as a walking holiday, did not quite turn out that way!

The following year we dragged my parents up to the area and repeated some of the visits before we were driven to cut short our stay, by both our son Adam and his Grandmother having violently upset stomachs!

At the end of 1976 I was moved by the Bank to Little Chalfont, in South Bucks, and we bought a house in Amersham. In retrospect, this proved to be a turning point.

Nothing dramatic happened initially. I spent some time viewing what had been the southern end of the Great Central – and trying to visualise A3s, B1s, etc, bowling through Little Chalfont and Amersham stations – and I looked at the Chesham branch, trying to picture aged ER C13s threading their way through the trees. In 1979 I picked up the camera again to record what was at Sheffield Park on the Bluebell Line, during a stay at the Bank's residential college in the Ashdown Forest. This spurred me to visit my new local preservation centre at Quainton Road in June 1979; and then, to keep up the interest, to take notes during our holiday visits to North Wales in July 1979 and 1980.

The Festiniog had by then extended to Tanygrisiau and, as well as bringing back memories of that brief trip with Gill, it was delightful to see a working railway again, albeit narrow gauge. Judith took an instant liking to the railway, partly due to the quaintness of the engines, but also because of its achievements and that it was run as a proper railway; and the children (Tammy had been born in 1978) enjoyed the rides, even at their young age, together with the sights of *Blanche*, *Prince* and *Merddin Emrys*.

But 1981 was *the* year of change. I had long since given up buying the railway press – being totally immersed in the music business instead – but I did keep half an eye on what was about. Due to increased pressures at work and constant domestic ties, Judith and I were not able to get out to concerts as we had in Leicester, and my outlets for music writing were falling away, as the music scene continued to change. Thus, the door that had opened at the end of steam was now closing. (Interestingly, both preoccupations lasted twelve years – 1956-68 and 1968-80.) This gave more fresh stimulus for railways and I snapped up a copy of a new magazine – *Railway Reflections* – which felt exactly as though it was the answer to some unspoken prayer and just what I had been waiting for.

The editor, Hugh Ramsey, lived not too far from me and we became firm friends. The dormant enthusiast within me was shaken and a passing comment from Hugh – that things change so quickly and that we should be recording it all, for tomorrow it would be gone – stirred me into action. I thought back to all those sights twenty years before: everyday scenes in Leicester which I had ignored photographically because they were so commonplace, that now I would give a ransom for; and I realised what I should be doing.

Like embers in a fire caught by a sudden breeze, I was fanned into a renewed blaze of enthusiasm and I had a direction again.

Early preservation scene, as love of steam dies hard

114. *Top* In those early days, I had to accept Industrial locos as those likely to be in steam. At Howarth, on 16 November 1968, No 31 stands in steam, in front of 'Black Five' 45212, whilst the latter receives some attention.

115. *Bottom* Almost steam from the chimney – but not quite! Prototype 'Crab' 42700 stands in the rain at Howarth, 16 November 1968.

116 & 117. Hard-earned Portuguese photos!
Above Metre-gauge No E85 pauses at Santo Tirso station, with
the driver detraining for he and his charge to be photographed,
18 May 1970. JUDI STRETTON

Below Another train bound for Oporto, leans into the curve
further down the line behind No E70, 23 May 1970.

118. *Above* Complaints were voiced against the Corporate Blue on diesels when work-stained. The maroon liveries fared little better, as can be seen from D1054 *Western Governor* and D832 *Onslaught* (*right*) on Penzance shed in August 1970. Blue-liveried D804 *Avenger*, behind D832, was slightly more presentable.

19. *Above* Much preservation work has equalled, if not surpassed, anything achieved by the original railways, especially externally. Ex-GWR Railcar 22 looks in magnificent condition, despite the dull conditions, at Bridgnorth in October 1972.

120 & 121. Two more examples of superb restoration.
Above Ex-GWR engines 6106 and 5322 – with a cheeky
headboard! – provide rides for an eager public at Didcot on 23
September 1973.

Below Beautifully restored 6100 *Royal Scot* also gives rides, but
this time on the footplate, creating misty conditions in the
overhanging trees at Bressingham, 16 September 1973.

Previous page
1. *Top* A very rare colour view of long-preserved MR118 and 158A, seen at Leicester & Midland Railway Exhibition held at Leicester (Belgrave Road) station from 19-30 June 1957. Admission was 6d (!) and the date is 20 June. DOUG GILES

2. *Bottom* In happier days, the unmistakeable brickwork of Swindon's A-Shop is backdrop to two spotless Westerns – D1035 *Western Yeoman* and D1013 *Western Ranger*, 10 May 1964.

3. *Top* I nearly missed getting this shot as, having chased the train by car through the streets of Perth, my camera strap wrapped itself around the steering wheel! Les, over the road got a closer view of 60031 *Golden Plover* leaving the town, bound for Dundee, 26 August 1964.

4. *Bottom* Later that same day, we spent a happy hour or two at Hilton Junction, just south of Perth, where the lines diverged for Glasgow or Edinburgh. D5327 and D5132 add a splash of colour as they pass the Junction Box, bound for Edinburgh.

5. *Top* A different view of Barry. Some kind soul had strategically chalked 2857's number at the end of a row stretching into the distance, 2 September 1964.

6. *Bottom* The station was closed, but the signal box remained (behind me in this view), seeing 48035 safely through Belgrave & Birstall station on its southward journey, 5 June 1965.

Early preserved steam.

7. *Top* I was still panting when I took this, having raced the train from Derby! In the late afternoon sun, 60019 *Bittern* heads south from the town at the head of a William's Deacóns Bank Club Special, 6 March 1966.

8. *Bottom* It was almost the crack of dawn, but it was worth it to be alone to see an immaculate 4472 *Flying Scotsman* head south through Thurmaston, towards Leicester, on 10 September 1966.

9. *Above* The shape of things to come. Prototype WCML electric, E3001, enters Crewe Station with a Euston-bound express from Manchester, 3 September 1967.

Overleaf

10. *Top* All the awnings and paraphernalia of these suburban platforms had disappeared within weeks of the picture being taken on my first visit to Watford. The Class 501 EMUs fared little better, with most going within three years. Here, a unit has just arrived from Euston in the evening sun of 15 May 1982.

11. *Bottom* What a romantic way to whisk your wife away on honeymoon! 31117 does the honours, on the *Wedding Belle*, leaving High Wycombe with the GW Saloon in tow – thought to be heading for Shrewsbury!? 23 June 1984.

12. *Above* Part of the scenery for so long, all has now gone. Leicester North Signal Box and its attendant semaphores were swept away with the closing of the Leicester Gap and the opening of the Power Box, (*being built extreme right*). This view is now bare and open. 30 September 1984.

Overleaf

13. *Top* The clouds, shadows and clean DMUs E54092 and E53135 make for a colourful scene at Leeds City, 14 March 1985.

14. *Bottom* Repainted as part of the GW150 celebrations, the brown and cream of W55020 is admired by the Stretton family at Reading Open Day, 1 June 1985.

122. *Top* Trainspotting leads to more than just collecting numbers. A love of, and interest in, railways generally, makes for times of great sadness when witnessing spectacles such as this at East Norton on the ex-GN&LNW joint line in Leicestershire, September 1973

123. *Bottom* Happily, a little line still survived near Parkend to give temporary home to 4150, in the bright sunshine of June 1974.

124. *Above* Chanced upon during our walk around York, preserved A3 4472 *Flying Scotsman* stops to take water at the station, giving time for admiration from small boys in June 1976

125. *Top right* 'Closely Observed Trains'! 'Big with child' Judith admires 1247, simmering quietly whilst waiting for the crossing gates at Grosmont to be opened, June 1976.

126. *Bottom right* Still on NYMR, but this time a year later, on 4 July 1977, Q6 2238 heads away from Grosmont in the hot afternoon sunshine, bound for Goathland, past a healthy load of washing!

127. *Above* The sun shines brightly, but the Bluebell Railway is quiet. 30064 stands with 1618 and other stock in various stages of restoration at Sheffield Park, 18 April 1979.

128 & 129. The Festiniog is undoubtedly one of the success stories of railway restoration and definitely appears as a working railway, rather than 'playing games'.

Top right 117-years old and still going strong, *Prince* runs round its train, at the then-terminus at Tanygrisiau, having lifted its train up the steep slopes from Porthmadog, 12 July 1980.
Bottom right A spring chicken by comparison – a mere 87-years old – *Blanche* sets off north out of Tan-y-Bwlch, 12 July 1980.

Early views, having steeled myself to diesels!

130. *Top* A Marylebone–Banbury service accelerates out of High Wycombe on 3 October 1981.

131. *Bottom* The fact that modern railways demand a more critical approach to achieve photographic success is amply shown by this view of 55016 *Gordon Highlander*, on the outward *Deltic Farewell* Special leaving Slough, 28 November 1981. Viewing this, I had to radically rethink my techniques!

CHAPTER SIX

The last five of these thirty years of my love affair with railways have seen dramatic changes on BR. Perhaps not as major as the extinction of steam or the Modernisation Plan, but just as drastic in many ways. There have been complete changes of thinking and approach at the top; directions have changed; whole Classes of motive power dispensed with; stations, lines and operating practices changed beyond all recognition; changing views on namings, liveries, slogans, main-line steam running, etc; and a whole shift of emphasis to the public. Scarcely a week has gone by, it seems, without some startling announcement or plan. My photography has also seen dramatic changes in equipment and approach over the years.

Coinciding with the rebirth of my interest was the death of the 'Deltics'. Strange, that I had witnessed their birth, elbowing out much-loved steam and now, here we were, seemingly only five minutes later, seeing their demise. In their latter years, they had become much loved and even the most disinterested party could hardly have failed to know about their passing, such was the ballyhoo and media coverage surrounding it all. Very late in the day, it was, but I was finally caught up in it dragging Adam and Tammy along to a very cold bridge in Slough where, quite some minutes late, on 28 November 1981, 55016 *Gordon Highlander* finally passed on the very last special. I duly photographed her and returned home somewhat mystified by the number!

1982 started quietly enough, with just two photographs of DMUs in Aylesbury station, taken from the car park as I was passing through; and then a visit to March depot – the first time for many years – in the twilight and early dark of 10 March, when en route from Southend to Nottingham, I took the numbers but, at that stage, they meant nothing to me. Sometime later, I would establish what was what and discover that I had copped 40176 (ex-D376), one of only three I needed from the old days. A good start!

But the photography was not so successful.

Mentally, I was still in steam days – very largely three-quarter views and point and shoot, not taking account of what exactly was in the frame. I had had the odd telegraph pole sticking out of boilers in steam days and without the romance and sheer aesthetic quality of steam, modern traction needed a whole new approach. This was reinforced by the 'Deltic' and March pictures which, for differing reasons, were very disappointing. I made a conscious effort to analyse what I was doing wrong, especially as this aspect of the hobby was becoming more important. Although again, very keen to capture the numbers, I was more eager to capture the sights on film and would be interested in snapping those things like DMUs, where I would not be recording the numbers for my collection.

One thing was immediately obvious – point and shoot was out and I soon learnt that the basic picture, without the train, had to be inherently pleasing if the shot was to be successful and satisfying. The addition of the actual train would be a 'bonus', the final icing on the cake.

Also, I could not 'follow' an engine, through the viewfinder and snap when I thought appropriate; it was necessary to focus on the point where I wanted the loco to be and then wait for it to get there! Finally, I swiftly came to the conclusion that I could not continue with just taking colour slides – as I had for the past twenty years; I would need to take black and white as well. This meant a second camera, an expense I could ill afford, especially as my existing one was now quite old – it was the same Pentacon SLR that I had bought secondhand in 1969 and the built-in lightmeter had failed some time ago! I scraped together enough to buy a Canon AE1-Program – then the very latest model – and thought that the automatic function would be the answer to all my prayers. Wrong again! Modern railway photography was proving far more difficult than I had at first realised and much harder than in steam days.

But I persevered and began taking the camera everywhere, even to the extent of breaking into shopping trips to sit in the car at Hemel Hempstead, taking photos through the windscreen in a rainstorm! Needless to say, the results were less than perfect and I realised that, despite the extra speeds, apertures and facilities on the camera – and the vastly improved film speeds and qualities – you still need decent light for a really clear photo.

Hot on the heels of the elimination of the 'Deltics', from the ECML by HSTs, the long familiar 'Peaks' (now Class 45) were to be pushed aside, in their turn, again by HSTs, at the beginning of September 1982. Having learnt from the experiences of the last days of steam, I travelled to Sandridge, north of St Albans, on

15 August to record some of the last scenes of 45s also the DMUs still working at the time, due only to the single-manning dispute that prevented the introduction of Bed-Pan electrics. Regrettably, my enthusiasm – and the two small children with me, on the edge of a cornfield! – overcame my photographic prowess and the potential of the trip was not realised. I was still having to learn, and disappointment was common; but there were so many things changing that I had plenty to practise on.

By 1981 Judith had begun taking a short holiday on her own, partly to escape the drudgery of domestic duties but, more importantly, to increase her interest in and knowledge of natural history. Wherever she went, she travelled by train, necessitating me acting as chauffeur to and from the relevant station. This suited me down to the ground, as I could both indulge my new-found passion and also take time out, whilst she was away and the kids were at school, to travel around the area, becoming more knowledgeable myself and increasing my photographic opportunities.

My emphasis now was to capture as much as possible and I had to work fast, as many of these changes came both quick and unexpected. On 15 May 1982, whilst Judith was waiting for her train, I snapped a 501 unit in the suburban platform of Watford station. Within a few months all the buildings on the platforms had been demolished in preparation for redevelopment. Shortly after this, I saw an architect's plan for the improvement of Watford's frontage and determined to photograph that before it disappeared; by the time I could get to the station, contractors' boards were everywhere. The pace of change had beaten me.

On 27 August Tammy was four, and on 2 September Adam was six. Disillusioned with birthday parties at home, we chose to take them out some-where with some of their friends. We chose 5 September as the day, and Didcot as the place. The weather was unkind, raining for much of the time, but the kids thoroughly enjoyed themselves, looking round all the engines and riding on the trains in the Great Western's site. Afterwards I found great pleasure in spotting from the car park by the station, while we all had birthday tea!

Since the early 70s, when I had lost most interest, new Classes had been introduced. I had already got to know the 87s, mostly from time spent at Watford, and HSTs were becoming more commonplace, but 56s were totally new to me. Spending Christmas back in Leicester, I continued to visit the old shed area and on New Year's Day 1983 I was intrigued at the sight of 56063, 56055, 56071, 56054, and 56048; I was also now sufficiently knowledgeable to know that Class 46 was also on the way out. I was pleased, therefore, to see 46017 present. Whilst in the area, I also retraced steps on the old GCR around Belgrave & Birstall station in order to take shots from vantage points previously seen in steam days, to create 'then-and-now' views. Even with the old prints in your hand, it is often excruciatingly difficult to stand in exactly the same position; and if you do, chances are the sun will be in the wrong direction, or that a tree, or some such, will

have sprouted over the years, blocking the view!

Having returned to reading the railway press, I was aware of many railtours, with locos in unusual locations. I had seen Metropolitan *Sarah Siddons* on a special at Amersham on 19 September 1982 (in the pouring rain), but the excitement of 1983 was to see *Flying Scotsman* return to the ECML on 27 February, on SLOA's *Scarborough Flyer*, the steam to run from Peterborough. Up till then, steam had only run on very few selected routes, most of which were out of reach; to see this was a real fillip and paved the way for BR to reconsider their refusals for many other routes.

Like the memorable month twenty years earlier, there was widespread snow on the day, leading to a cold and messy walk to the embankment at Burton Coggles. Trying to find a decent vantage point for the all-important photograph was difficult, as there were like-minded bodies everywhere – and many were where they most definitely should not have been! Having set up their tripods on the assumption that the train would be on the main lines, at the cry: 'She's on the slow line', there was a hurried migration by a certain mindless minority to the opposite embankment – straight across the running tracks, almost without looking, with 125mph HSTs due any time! And then, they were the wrong side for the sun!

This incident crystallised thoughts in my mind. I did not want to be linked with the lunatic fringe in the hobby – I had always tried to act responsibly, even from the very earliest days; and I was really more interested in photographing the modern scene.

In view of my feelings in 1968, at the end of steam, this was perhaps unexpected; but, although it had been nice to see *Scotsman* out on the main line and it was pleasing to see the various locos up and down the country in the preservation centres, all of their junketings were artificial. What I missed about the old days was the reality of a working railway and that is what I now wanted to capture, before any parts of it disappeared. David had different views, favouring steam, and he could not understand my stance; we were to have many discussions on the matter!

Not that I ignored the Centres entirely, as visits to Didcot on 6 March and to Butterley on 23 March testified, but they did not totally satisfy. What did, though, was a trip to Broad Street on 4 March.

Strangely, I had never visited the station before, despite various visits to Liverpool Street next door, but on this day it was like stepping back in time. Largely deserted and much of it unused and overgrown, it had a feeling of the steam era still about it, especially with the signal box at the end of the platform; and, although the motive power was 501 units, that feeling of peace, so prevalent all those years before, came sweeping back. I was quite sad to leave and walk back to the 20th century and the bustle of Liverpool Street; I was back at Broad Street on 22 April and that would not be my last time.

On 5 June, with the children, I met up with David once more, at Aynho, supposedly to photograph a steam special. Having trekked a mile to our vantage point – a farm bridge, that we were sharing with a herd of cows! – we learnt that the trip had been cancelled!

The day was hot and we did not appreciate the long walk back, but we were consoled (or at least I was), by the sight of a couple of expresses, before making our way for a visit to Didcot. Six days later, I spent time at Watford awaiting Judith's return and I was rewarded with a whole succession of trains. Once more, the station was due to change shortly and the photos that day were very soon historic.

But I was missing the tours. Making my own brief sorties was one thing – and I did derive enormous pleasure from them – but I yearned for the organised trip. I was to get some satisfaction on 16 June.

The Bank's Oxford District Manager's Assistant's Club arranged a trip to Swindon Works. Although working at the other end of the District, I made sure of my place. Most of the others were idly interested in railways and the engineering side, seen inside the Works, but there was one other who was as keen as I to collect the numbers and walk the scrap yard. Like me, Paul was interested in the modern scene and, like me, he had his camera with him. We were 'on pain of death' not to take shots in the scrap yard (as BR was sensitive of their image!?) but our guide never seemed to be looking at the appropriate moments! Secretly snapping, Paul and I felt just a little like industrial spies!

By this time I had been commissioned by a publisher to put together a railway photographic book. Wanting to see some of David's photos for possible use, I travelled to Notts to see what he could offer. One thing he did offer was a trip to Toton – a proper shed visit at last! Now I was in seventh heaven. As well as 56s, 20s, 45s, 25s, 31s, 08s, 40s, 46s and 47s – and as if that were not enough – there were the 58s. Only recently introduced, they were a fascinating revelation, with a new body design but, more significantly, in Railfreight livery. A totally new concept at the time, it spread prolifically over the next few years and, despite my early fears on the matter, the livery did actually survive the daily grime and vagaries of our weather remarkably well. But by far the coup of this visit was the surprise of seeing 40122 on shed.

Not really expecting to see a 40 at all, although they did work in on occasions, I had been pleased to see 40076 in the yard; but that was nothing to our joint surprise when entering the shed building – on the lookout for the foreman at the same time! – we saw 40122 in grey undercoat, (see plate 138). Neither of us knew it before our visit, but it was being restored to its persona as D200 and Toton had the job of restoration. That foreman stood by the engine, but he was (fortunately) entirely sympathetic to our feelings and allowed photos of the undertaking. Also on shed was ADB968002 – ex-D8237; truly, it had been a visit of variety and surprises.

By now the bug had really bitten again and I and my camera went everywhere we could. On holiday in Buxton in July, I made nightly pilgrimages to the shed; where 45s, 40s, 37s and 47s were all seen in number; and I dragged Judith and the children to Dinting to espy the preservation scene there; and then, on 29 August – ostensibly as a birthday treat for Adam and Tammy – I dragged them all, plus Mum and Dad, on a railtour!

Having come to know the organiser of the LNER Society, I booked on a trip to York, joining the train at the seemingly unearthly hour of 7am at Hemel Hempstead. I found the trip fascinating, by way of Nuneaton (change of locomotion and reversal), Leicester, Derby and Sheffield; but the others took it with varying degrees of favour! A nice sight was preserved Black Five No 5305, steamed up and ready to go, on the day's *Scarborough Spa Express*. The photos I took in those first few minutes, before this excursion departed, were fortuitous as the engine failed a mere 5 miles out of York! This did delay our return train a little, as we had to wait for those Society members who had travelled to Scarborough, but 45108 did sterling work on the return run and we were right time by Nuneaton (where 86004 took over).

The rest of 1983 was taken up with a variety of odd trips to all manner of places for all manner of reasons, but always with the camera ever ready. It came in useful on 23 December, when I sped from Little Chalfont to Hemel Hempstead in my lunch hour, to record the wrong line workings. News had reached me that a freight had brought down the wires in the station area on the slow lines and that in consequence all trains were working on the fast lines. This meant that paths had to be found between expresses for the locals and freight trains, with inevitable delays. I only had roughly 35mins to record the scene, but it was all go, and well worth the trip.

I was now learning to keep my ears open for news of developments; to keep my eyes open and scan the press for likely opportunities; and to keep my options open, by visiting as much and as often, places that otherwise seemed to offer little. Thus, by opportunistically walking to Little Chalfont station in the lunch-break of 4 January 1984, I was rewarded by the sight of two sets of, as yet undelivered, stock for the Victoria line, being given brake test runs. Loading them with sand bags, etc – to simulate passengers – new stock was run out to the Amersham line for such tests, as they could get a decent run between stations and then slam on the brakes, with little danger of any overshooting or running into anything. But the undoubted highlight of 1984, to date, was my next LNER Society trip to Glasgow on 3 March.

This was pure trainspotting, with me entraining at Hemel Hempstead, to be joined by Hugh at Bletchley and David at Rugby. We travelled north through Crewe – collecting numbers like mad things as we went! – and then via Blackburn and Hellifield, to reach the Settle & Carlisle line. The closure notice had been posted and it was widely rumoured and expected that 1984 would be the last year. We all felt that we had to make an effort to travel the line for possibly the last time and we were graced, on the outward run, with brilliant sunshine. The sun on the snow around Ribblehead was quite breathtaking, as was the cold when leaning out of the carriage windows, for photos!

Through Carlisle, we had a double bonus of a run over the G&SW route to Glasgow. Here, nothing was planned by the Society, so we three hopped into a taxi for an impromptu visit to Eastfield. The shed foreman was somewhat suspicious of my blanket permit – for Scottish sheds – but, with a donation to the railwaymen's fund, he allowed us to tour the area.

With 46 engines present, we were treated to a very successful visit and, just before rain set in, were able to photograph – and in Hugh's case, video – the shed scene. Although diesel, it was 'reality', with the engines being workhorses and nothing artificial about any of them. Also, although we did not know it then, it would be the last time that I would see Class 27s in working order. We also had our first sight of ETHEL 3 (ex-25319), a loco especially modified to provide electric train heating.

One thing that did surprise us in the taxi ride to the shed was the sight of a car blazing merrily away in a sidestreet. Passers-by – and, indeed, children playing nearby – seemed totally unperturbed by it! When quizzed, the taxi driver merely commented that this was a poor part of the city and that it was an everyday occurrence! After that, the woman stopping the return journey at Preston because she had smelt burning and thought the train was on fire seemed tame by comparison!

The beauty of trips, now, as much as seeing the engines, was the facility and relative cheapness of 36 exposures film; luxury, compared to the trips to Scotland, twenty years earlier, when I had gone with just two films of 12 exposures each for the whole week! Now I thought nothing of running off a whole reel on one shed. And the much faster film speeds, vastly improved camera facilities, and even improved film emulsions, meant that I could snap away without counting the numbers. Thus, the number of films I was getting through was rapidly increasing.

In April 1984 I was again moved by the Bank, this time to Flackwell Heath – very close to the High Wycombe-Marylebone line! I quickly learnt of the 1740 Paddington-Wolverhampton service and its return working the next morning. The latter reached Loudwater, the point nearest the branch, at around 8.40am. On my way to work, and just in time before being due at work, I made a point of seeing this as often as possible, as it was the only loco-hauled train, over what had been the GWR Birmingham-Paddington main line. Now single track from Princes Risborough to Bicester, it only saw DMUs for passengers and especially as it was rostered for a Class 50 – otherwise unknown on the line – it was a must photograph, (see Plate 157). There were many funny looks from the locals, as I stood by the line so early in the morning, camera poised – especially as, most of the time, I was attired somewhat like a spaceman, in motorcycle gear!

I was now looking for trips to make, usually on my own, and was experimenting with enhancements to my cameras – (I now had a second AE1-Program) – with zooms and filters. Some shots were very successful but these were new techniques that I had to conquer. I took to dashing to Taplow – on the WR main line – in my lunch-hour, to record as much as I could; and on 7 June I made what would prove to be my last successful trip to Broad Street, to photo the 501s on the service to Richmond and Watford, before they and the station disappeared for ever.

It was now becoming a race to capture scenes before they vanished, almost before my eyes; as well as the one-off specials, which were becoming more popular and widespread. In the latter vein there was *The Wedding Belle*, on 23 June, taking a honeymoon couple on their first trip as a married pair, from High Wycombe to, it was rumoured, Shrewsbury, behind 31117. How many husbands, I wonder, have ever thought of hiring a complete train, to whisk away their bride? Then there was 1054, on a Wilson's Brewery 150th Anniversary special, at Manchester Victoria on 1 August (seen by Tammy and I, as we interrupted our current holiday in Buxton) and there was our family visit to Quainton Road on 26 August.

Having had my book of photographs published in July, the local press wanted a story. I was dragged kicking and screaming (!?) to Quainton Road, for a series of photographs in all sorts of poses and disguises – shovelling the coal on the footplate, waving the flag from the Guard's Van, etc. I must own to feeling somewhat ridiculous, but the finished product, published with the appropriate articles, looked fine – and it was all in a good cause!

I made frequent re-visits to Leicester to see parents and friends but on 30 September made a first trip to Vic Berry's Scrap Yard, in Western Boulevard, where I was fascinated to see the delightful 03 shunter, 03069, recently bought from BR and used for shunting stock around the yard. I was also intrigued that day to see in Leicester depot yard 82004 and 82006! Bound for Vic's yard, they were, to my knowledge, the first electrics to be seen on Leicester shed. There were more to follow, in the next few months, as 82s and 83s were brought for scrapping, and over the next two years I would return to the Vic Berry site on many occasions.

1985 dawned with big news – steam was to return to Marylebone.

For the twenty years since the demise of steam on the Great Central, BR had staunchly and stubbornly refused to admit preserved steam back to the terminus, trotting out a number of dubious reasons why. Suddenly, it now suited their purpose, in order to help publicise the issue of a set of railway stamps. Therefore, on a bitterly cold late afternoon on 12 January, Tammy and I stood on the ice of Beaconsfield's platform, to see 4498 *Sir Nigel Gresley* steam sedately through the station, at the head of the *Thames-Avon Pullman* – 45mins late! In the ensuing months/years, her resplendent blue livery would be seen often, on the Sunday specials to Stratford-upon-Avon; as would also in succession: 35028 *Clan Line*, 46229 *Duchess of Hamilton*, 30777 *Sir Lamiel*, 34092 *City of Wells*, 4422 *Mallard* and 4771 *Green Arrow*. Wherever (and whenever) the trains went, there were hundreds of photographers lineside, and a good many of these were armchair photographers, crawling out of the woodwork, their interests re-awakened. It became difficult to find a vantage point free of other bodies – a problem now common to steam routes throughout the country.

As can be seen in previous chapters, one of the pleasant spin-offs of railway enthusiasm is the frequent camaraderie and common bonding. Friends are quickly and easily made and this was reinforced when, on 12 March, I stole away from a party of Bank Ten-Pin bowlers in Manchester for the day, to visit Victoria and Piccadilly stations. At the former, a conversation struck up with a highly knowledgeable spotter led to an invitation to join him on a visit to Newton Heath shed. Neither of us having a permit, we were brazen and talked our way round and were rewarded by the sight of 56066 – of Toton shed – on crew training. Also, on depot, were some of the ex-St Pancras DMUs, displaced by the Bed-Pan electrics and sent north for conversion to parcels cars. Again, the surprises had come when least expected and reinforced the adage, 'if it's there, photograph it'. Many such scenes – so obviously, in retrospect – have been totally unrepeatable.

On 10 April I went to Tring station to photo the APT, which was running regular trial trips, from Crewe to Euston and was due through the station at lunchtime. With Judith away and Tammy playing close to me on the platform, I set up the camera on tripod. Having checked with the station 'master' the time at which it was due, he kindly provided coffee while we chatted and waited. He even checked back up the line when it was late. It began to be later and later and unfortunately at 1.30pm I had to call it a day. We piled into the car and drove away from the station – only to see the wretched thing roar through as we did so! It was due back in the early evening, so all was not lost – I thought. Having established when it was due back through Tring, I arranged my day, to be back there in time. I was, but the APT chose to be early; it was approaching as I, in turn, approached my vantage point. I had no time to do other than stop the car, grab the camera and snap; no time to check exposures, speeds, anything! The photo turned out, but only just – I was fated not to get it then and I never saw it again. To say I was frustrated was to put it mildly!

Other travels were more successful.

On 1st June the whole family – Mum and Dad included – went to Reading Open Day, graced by brilliant and hot sunny weather. The first such event since the days of Derby and Brush, it was most enjoyable and everyone derived great pleasure from the day and delights such as a brief trip behind peserved 5572. On 16 June I travelled through Victoria, on the way to a Bank course, and captured shots of the Gatwick Expresses; Buxton was again revisited from 21 July and we sampled the joys of the first year's Peak Rail Rambler service to New Mills Central and back; and Toton was once more visited on 18 August. Old Oak Common Open Day was an event not to miss, on 15 September; accompanied by friend and fellow-banker, Richard, Adam and I arrived early in the day when the sun still shone, and the sight of 6000 *King George V* and the reconstructed *Iron Duke* on adjacent tracks was good to see, as were 46229 in steam and preserved D7018 and D1015 inside the shed buildings – despite the thronging crowds

preventing satisfying photographs. Richard was very knowledgeable about London's railways and, through his sound advice, I travelled part of the North London line, from Stratford to Gospel Oak. Not only was this virgin territory for me, it also provided me with a new set of locations for photos and, graced again with good weather, achieved the results that often come from impromptu affairs and often do not come from hours of preparation. Once more, that serenity of feeling, descended on me.

1986's events opened, for me, with a railtour undertaken with a new friend. Mike had never been on a train trip just for the sheer fun of the trip itself – he had always previously used rail as a means to an end. Would he enjoy it? With snow thick everywhere and the train – *The Derbyshire Dingle*, of 8 February – nearly an hour late at High Wycombe (it's first stop out of London!), the omens did not look good. But the day went superbly, with 50016 *Barham* and then 50012 *Benbow* (from Derby) performing faultlessly, and to see a 50 at both Buxton and Manchester Piccadilly, was a treat indeed.

Wokingham station was next, on 14 March, when I again went AWOL from a Ten-Pin bowling party. After this I was moved by the Bank once more, this time to Faringdon. Involving a move of house, it also meant a host of new locations; and I would be close to Swindon. Unfortunately, this latter was not to be the bonus that it once would have been, as closure of the Works had already been announced and programmed. I was too late for the pace of change once more – story of my life! I did, however, see much of what was still there at the time, before it was either cut up on site, or transferred away for disposal.

The new area gave me new places to find and photograph, such as the Kintbury/Hungerford stretch, where I saw and photographed my first 59s. Christened 'The Quiet Americans' by local railmen at Swindon, they were certainly very impressive locos and well worth the effort to capture them on film. The move also gave me the opportunities for fresh fields in the months that I travelled back and forth between Faringdon and Amersham, before we actually moved house. But *the* absolute highlight of the whole year was on 28 May when, courtesy of *Railscene*, I was treated to a cab-ride in an HST, from St Pancras to Sheffield. A double thrill – being both in the cab and over the line I knew so well, through Leicester – it was the dream of a lifetime and an unfulfilled ambition. The trip was both spectacular and unspectacular! The former was from the totally new slant on the views of a well-known line; and the latter due to the sheer professional and trouble-free rides given by both driver and HST set.

After that, everything else seemed so tame; but that did not stop me continually getting out and about at every conceivable opportunity, and the year ended with a deliberate direct journey from Reading to Gatwick – rather than through London – to reach Hayward's Heath from Swindon, so that I could sample and photograph that line. Unfortunately, I chose a Sunday – 8 September – when there were engineering works, causing delays, diversions and missed connections – but I finally made my destination and the journey, through unexpected locations, was worth it!

Looking back as the year ended, so much had changed over the five years since the rekindling – whole Classes disappearing or on the verge of extinction; stations and lines closed or under threat but, also, many more opened or re-opened; new liveries; changes of mind along the corridors of power; wholesale re-numberings and sub-classes created; ambivalent and often weird naming policies; old names disappearing from the scene – Stockton, Swindon, etc; and the asbestos scares. To come within months was the elimination of Classes 25 and 27; the imminent elimination of 03s and 45s; Class 50s and 47s being withdrawn; Network South-East; a whole proliferation of liveries, including a Railfreight rethink; yet more more stations and services; the proposals for Classes 60, 90 and 91; plus much more.

It has become impossible to see more than the tip of the iceberg myself – such is the pace of change and development – and, therefore, the emergence, over the past few years, of a healthy railway video scene is applauded and encouraged.

So, the thirty years ended with as much enthusiasm within me as when it began. Much has happened on the way; much has changed, not least my perception and approach to the hobby; many of us have had to re-assess our photographic approaches but, still, the potential for enjoyment, satisfaction and gratification is as great as ever. Railways never cease to satisfy, stimulate, amuse and challenge me. To those not imbued with the same enthusiasm – in whatever direction – I genuinely feel sorry, as its end result is so rewarding and adds so much to my life.

And looking back over thirty years, I think I have proved Dad wrong!

132. *Top* A fresh eye, using what's there and the prevailing weather (see the raindrops on the trolley handle). Almost timeless, this was a summer (!) scene at Hemel Hempstead on 19 June 1982.

133. *Bottom* Such are the strides in preservation and recreation that a mail pick-up is re-created, with 506 *Butler Henderson* really looking the part, at speed, about to grab mail at Quorn, on 30 October 1982

134. *Above* Over the New Year weekend of 1983, the GCR held a 60th Anniversary Celebration of the Grouping of 1923. 4744 worked all services and is seen on the first train of the day – 11.45 Loughborough-Rothley – passing the site originally proposed for Swithland station (never built), 2 January 1983.

135. *Top right* I had only got to know Broad Street station very late in its life, when it was in imminent danger of closure. The overall train shed has all but gone and the platform area to the left of this shot was covered in weeds, but the services to Richmond and Watford survived and the 16.41 train to the latter destination is about to leave, 22 April 1983.

136. *Bottom right* If anyone was in any doubt as to the devotion to diesels, this 'homage' should enlighten them! The 'revered' is 47422 at Liverpool Street, on 22 April 1983.

137. *Above* A scene once so common and now no more. 08795 and 08778 receive attention inside Swindon's famous A-Shop, now a wasted resource, 16 June 1983.

138. *Top right* This sight was a complete surprise and the click of my camera shutter brought us to the attention of the foreman (*centre*). Fortunately, he was sympathetic to our appreciation of the work on D200 (still 40122 at the time) returning her to green, and we were allowed closer inspection of the hand painting. Toton, 17 July 1983.

139. *Bottom right* Some of the relief and expectation can be seen, as a delayed return LNER Society Special slides gently into York station behind 45108. The run through Sheffield and Leicester was so good that right time was achieved at Nuneaton, where 45108 was replaced for the electric run to Euston, 29 August 1983.

140 & 141. Opposite ends of the country.

Top In pouring rain, 27042 stands outside Eastfield depot, 3 March 1984. (The journey to Glasgow had been in brilliant sunshine!)

Bottom Looking as though in conversation, HST power cars 43166 and 43009 are refuelled at Paddington, 7 June 1984.

142. *Top* Still in all-blue livery, but very well kept, Class 104
DMU M53598 prepares to receive its crew for the 1418 trip to
Buxton at Manchester Piccadilly, 1 August 1984. Behind are 108
No M59390 and 104 No M53542.

143. *Bottom* A fast disappearing class at the time, 40091 was a
surprise sight, pushing two DMU coaches through Manchester
Piccadilly, towards Longsight, on 1 August 1984. Note the two
sets of non-standard numbers on her nose.

144. *Above* Quainton Road station on 26 August 1984 and GWR 7715 arrives with a train, viewed past SR E0314 awaiting restoration.

145. *Top right* One of the views during a lunchtime escape from work. 50045 *Achilles* trundles a short load of new deliveries towards London, through Taplow Station, on 3 September 1984

146. *Bottom right* HST 43088 with the motors ticking over, waits for the right of way, to form the 1330 express to Sheffield. St Pancras, 28 October 1984.

147. *Above* The one that restarted it all for Marylebone. The
Royal Mail Special, hauled by 47500 *Great Western* – still in blue
livery and with facsimile stamps on the bodyside – drifts through
Beaconsfield station, on 22 January 1985. Within days, steam
had reappeared at Marylebone for the first time for twenty
years.

148. *Right* The second steam to grace the Sunday excursions out
of Marylebone was 35028 *Clan Line*. On one of her early runs,
thankfully and rarely without headboard, she approaches West
Wycombe on 10 March 1985.

Time out from a Ten-Pin Bowling Tour!

149. *Top left* To visit Manchester Victoria, where Class 128
Motor Parcels Van M55993 hides away in the suburban platforms,
12 March 1985.

150. *Bottom left* To spend time at Leeds City, where 08503 is
seen pushing 47157 through the station area in bright sunshine,
14 March 1985.

151. *Above* In the last few years Vic Berry has acquired renown
for the number of locos handled by his scrapyard in Leicester.
To move the stock around the yard, he bought 03069 from BR;
it is seen here in fine condition on 6 April 1985.

152. *Top* On the evening of 30 April 1985, 35028 *Clan Line* ran a one-off Special from Marylebone-Stratford-upon-Avon, with D200 due to work the return leg. In bright sunshine she bursts from Wooburn Moor Tunnel, between Beaconsfield and High Wycombe.

153. *Bottom* Four days after the above, 46229 *Duchess of Hamilton* was a very welcome visitor to ex-GCR metals. She worked south on the *South Yorkshireman* Special and is seen – bang on time – working down the bank towards Saunderton on 4 May 1985.

154 & 155. Two views of endangered Class 25s.
Top 25302 had a final moment of glory, at Reading Open Day on 1 June 1985, in company with 58004; she worked no more, however, being withdrawn immediately afterwards.

Bottom Suitably seen in twilight, 25213 was subsequently named *Castell Y Waun/Chirk Castle* and, despite the evidence of collision damage, survived to the end of the Class, being withdrawn on 19 March 1987. Seen here at Buxton 26 July 1985.

156. *Top* A view of the ex-Great Central main line on 18 August 1985, looking south, towards the old shed area.

157. *Bottom* It was a race between this train – the 0622 Wolverhampton-Paddington – and my motorbike every morning to reach this spot. On 14 August 1985 I won and captured 50011 *Centurion*, working up the bank out of High Wycombe, past Loudwater; this was to be the first Class 50 to be withdrawn.

158. *Top* My first purely enthusiast's trip for many years on 8 February 1986. 50016 *Barham* heads the *Derbyshire Dingle* (already over 30mins late!) through the snow into High Wycombe station, past a London-bound DMU and under a delightful selection of signals.

159. *Bottom* In the evening of 1 May 1986 the lowering sun nicely picks out the details on the wagons trailing behind 37232, passing Longcot, east of Swindon, on a 'down' freight.

160. *Top* A very rare sight: a Hastings unit on the ex-GC main line, approaching Amersham. Having split earlier in the day from another unit, No 1032 passes Windmill Wood on the return leg of the *Farewell Tour* of 11 May 1986.

161. *Bottom left* Following the demise of other Classes and their expulsion from express duties by HSTs, Class 45s began to be withdrawn in numbers during 1985-6. Survivor 45007 stands at St Pancras, having brought in empty stock 28 May 1986.

162. *Bottom right* The end for so many. Both cabs of 25284 face forlornly outwards at the end of this row, in company with Class 40s and 45s. Vic Berry's scrapyard has claimed more, 28 December 1986.